How to Use
Journey
▲

www.TheJourneyForum.com

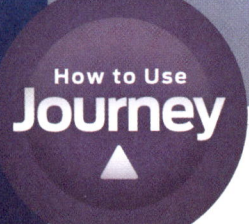

Congratulations in starting Journey.

1. Register
Go to www.TheJourneyForum.com and click on "Users" to register and see the free resources available for you. Every page of every lesson has resources on the website.

2. Look in Journey
Next, look at the Table of Contents page to see the subjects we will study. Then look at the last few pages of Journey, at the Steps of Discipleship and the Destinations of our Journey. Seeing these characteristics come true in our lives is the purpose for Journey.

3. Procedures
Journey gets its best results by meeting one on one. Men meet with men. Women with women. And the church leadership decides who meets with whom. Close family members and best friends should only meet together with their Pastor's approval.

Meet together at least once every week and if there are times you can't, schedule "catch-up" meetings. If you meet every day, study the lessons in Journey only every 2 or 3 days for the teaching to be absorbed more; use the other days to learn from the Daily in the Word assignments (discussed in Lesson 2.) Never have long periods of time where you don't meet together. Many use the internet or telephone to stay connected when they have to be apart. It's very important to keep your conversations confidential unless something is life threatening or very serious. It's also important that the disciple only work on the lessons with their Discipler and not in advance. The disciple can read the Bible verses that will be studied in advance but should not write answers in the blanks ahead of a meeting. Disciplers should not add their own materials or topics. If you're a disciple, ask questions at any time. The Discipler may need to prepare an answer for your question or tell you that the answer is coming in a future lesson. Journey is designed for you to grow in God's Word together.

4. Lesson One
Understand that Lesson One is designed to lead people to Christ or to teach a disciple a complete study on Salvation. You can begin Journey with a believer or non-believer.

5. A Typical Discipleship Meeting
When meeting together, first take time to talk to each other. There are times you will not even open the lessons but always encourage one another with the Word of God. Then you normally exchange your Daily in the Word and other assignments to see how each of you is doing (you'll see these assignments in each lesson.) The Discipler reviews and signs that they were completed.

Then the Discipler prays before starting the lesson. Review what you have learned before starting new subjects. The Discipler reads any introductions and summaries and the disciple reads the Bible verses. Sometimes the Discipler will read verses they want to emphasize. The Discipler reads the comments and gives the answers for the blanks and the disciple writes the answers in their lesson.

The Discipler prepares for the lesson by knowing the context of the Bible verses and the meaning of key words in the verses you will study. You will see an "icon" on the left side of many pages. This indicates that there are some additional thoughts we want the Discipler to know about in that section. You can find the information on the web site. There are guiding instructions built into the lessons. As you come to them, just follow the instructions. Start at the beginning and do not skip any section, page, or assignment.

At the end of each section, do what's asked in the Reflect and Transfer. The Reflect and Transfer is designed to review and internalize the important teachings. Answer each question. Do all the assignments and activities assigned at the end of each lesson.

The Discipler reviews what you have learned when it is time to end. Then schedule your next meeting and record your meeting in your records (see your church leaders for their record keeping method.) Close the meeting with prayer. If you need more training, visit the web site; new items are added regularly. Thank you.

Congratulations again and may God multiply disciple makers through you.
John and Cathy Honeycutt

Table of Contents

Lesson One

Theme: Salvation
Topics: Creation and the one true God
The triune God
Where evil came from
The first man and woman
Sin and the love and grace of God
The promise of a Saviour
The Saviour revealed
The Ten Commandments
The claims of the Saviour
Good works and salvation
How to receive salvation
Commitment to salvation

Lesson Two

Theme: Assurance of salvation
Topics: The meaning of assurance
The reliability of the Word of God
The author of the Bible
Enemies of the Bible
The promises in the Word of God
God's Holy Spirit dwells in us
Salvation is secure
Your new relationship with God

Lesson Three

Theme: Prayer
Topics: Knowing God through prayer
Why pray
How to pray
When to pray
Answers to prayer
The Lord's Prayer
Hindrances to prayer
Sin after salvation

Lesson Four

Theme: Local Church
Topics: The beginning of the church
Functions of the local church
Responsibility to the church
Purpose of Biblical leadership
Dynamic role of women in the church
Importance of baptism
Baptism and salvation
The need for baptism

Lesson Five

Theme: Discipleship
Topics: Steps of discipleship
Cost of discipleship
Commitment to discipleship
Destination of spiritual formation
Stewardship of our lives
Giving and the disciple

Discipleship Training Module 1
Topic: The definition of one on one discipleship

Lesson Six

Theme: The Future
Topics: Our spiritual struggle
Our spiritual armor
The end of the struggle
The rapture
The tribulation
The second coming
The millennium
The new heaven and new earth
The judgment seat of Christ

Discipleship Training Module 2
Topic: The value of one on one discipleship

Lesson Seven

Theme: Spiritual Growth
Topics: Our culture today
Importance of holiness
Principles of purity
Seven stages of spiritual growth

Discipleship Training Module 3 & 4
Topic: Procedures for one on one discipleship
The Value of discipleship

Lesson Eight

Theme: Faith
Topics: Understanding faith
Trial and testing
Heroes of the faith
The Holy Spirit

Discipleship Training Module 5 & 6
Topics: Before accepting a disciple
Getting started with your new disciple

Lesson Nine

Theme: Words
Topics: Problem solving with Christians
Understanding false teachers
How to answer non-Christian beliefs
Drawing people to Christ

Discipleship Training Module 7
Topic: Your strategy in discipleship

Lesson Ten

Theme: Loving God
Topics: The greatest commandment
A new commandment
Go and make disciples

Salvation
LESSON 1

SALVATION THROUGH CHRIST. GOD THE FATHER. THE HOLY SPIRIT. HOLINESS. SIN. GRACE. MERCY. UNDESERVED FAVOR. THE MERCY SEAT. AT THE RIGHT HAND OF THE FATHER

SECTION A

LESSON 1 — Salvation

The Beginning

Key Objective: To understand the one true God of the Bible.

Did you know that the Bible addresses the foundational questions of life - whether asked in an intellectual setting or discussed by people at the water cooler?

Let's see what the Bible says about who God is, who we are, our purpose, the source of all problems, and the solution to those problems. The Bible's truth is for everyone.

If you have major questions still unanswered, I suggest that you approach this study honestly with an attitude that says, "God, I want to know if You exist and why I am here. If You are there, help me to be willing to humble myself before You."

- **Genesis 1:1**

  The One True _____ made everything. He not only _____ the world, but the heavens and the earth-everything there is.

- **Psalms 33:6, 9**

  God created all things out of nothing. He spoke and it was. And His creation has its own separate _____ from God; He does not exist in the trees, rocks, or earth.

- **Revelation 4:11**

  God is _____ in Himself. God did not have to create but He wanted to receive _____ from all He created.

- **Genesis 1:31**

  After God had created all things, He pronounced it "_____ _____." All things were completely good as they were originally made. This is because God is perfectly _____ and completely _____.

  We can see that God _____ with a thought out plan.

God was and is and will always be.

- **Ephesians 2:4**

  God not only thinks and acts, He _____. Therefore the God who exists is _____. He thinks, acts, and feels… three marks of personality. God is not simply a force nor is He in everything that exists. He is a person. And God created us to have a _____ relationship with him.

SECTION A

Mark 12:32

Though people may believe there are other _____, the Bible teaches there is only one God.

Maybe you have wondered why some people use the words Father, Jesus, and Spirit for God? To understand why, let's learn about the nature of God:

Genesis 1:26

"**Let us make man in our image.**" Here it is shown that there is more than one _____ in what the Bible refers to as the "Godhead." (See **Acts 17:29**)

- **1st John 5:7**

  In this verse, each of the _____ persons is clearly seen.

  Notice God the Father:

- **1st Corinthians 8:6**

  God the _____ is God and is shown as separate and distinct from the other persons of the Godhead.

  Notice God the Son:

- **John 1:1-3, 14**

  These verses state that the person called "the _____" is God and made all things. Verse 14 shows that "the Word" is Jesus Christ. Jesus Christ is _____ God. He is God in a human body.

- **Matthew 9:1-7**

  Jesus Christ claims the power of _____ sins as His natural right, thus showing that He claims to be _____. Only the Holy God can forgive sins.

The one true God is a Triune God.

Notice God the Holy Spirit:

- **Acts 5:3-4**   These verses show that lying to the Holy Spirit is lying to God.

- **Acts 16:6**   The Holy Spirit _____ and He _____.

- **Ephesians 4:30**

  This verse shows that the Holy Spirit also _____. The Holy Spirit is not a force but is a person; He thinks, acts, feels, and is active in comforting our lives.

SECTION A

- **2nd Corinthians 13:14**

    All persons of the Godhead are seen in this verse. To summarize, there is one true God and He is triune, as the three in one.

    Now let's learn about the beginning of evil in the world:

    Revelation 5:11-12

    God created many wonderful and beautiful _____ before He created the first man and woman. Angels were created to do God's will, worship Him and serve Him. A very special angel, named _____ , was the most beautiful angel because God's Glory would shine through him.

- **Isaiah 14:12-15**

    Lucifer _____ against God. Lucifer wanted to share God's power and glory. Because of his rebellion, God cast him out of Heaven.

- **Revelation 12:9**

    Lucifer is now known as "the Serpent ", "the Devil "or "Satan". He lost the beauty and light he once had and became _____ and full of _____. Many of the angels joined in his rebellion and were cast out with Lucifer.

    1st Corinthians 10:19-20

    Demons are the false _____ that are worshipped by people around the world. They are represented by _____. The Scriptures teach that the only spirit beings other than the one true God are the angels of God, the Devil and his evil spirits.

    Some of the names of Lucifer are "Satan" which means adversary and the "Devil" which means slanderer. Other titles and names are:

- **Matthew 13:38**   The _____ one

- **2nd Corinthians 4:4**   Lucifer is the _____ of this world.

- **1st Thessalonians 3:5**   Another name for Lucifer is the _____.

    Notice how Satan continues to work today:

- **Genesis 3:1-4**   Perverting the _____ of God

- **2nd Corinthians 11:4**   In _____

- **1st Thessalonians 2:17-18**   Hindering God's _____

- **Revelation 12:9**   _____ people

SECTION A

- **Matthew 25:41** and **Revelation 20:10**

  Hell will be the Devil's place forever when God _____ all sin.

- **Psalms 99:5**

  God will judge sin one day because He is supremely holy, pure, and without any evil and cannot excuse any _____.

  In summary, the Bible teaches us that evil began when Lucifer rebelled against God.

- **Genesis 2:7**

  In this verse we learn that God _____ the body of the first man out of the dust of the ground. However; man is more than a _____.

- **Genesis 1:26-27**

  Man was made in God's _____ and likeness. God made us with a body, soul and spirit (three in one) and this sets us apart from other creatures. What does it mean that man is made in God's image? Among other things, it means people have a sense of right and wrong, which means we can make _____ and think for ourselves. It also means that people are creative. Men and women in all parts of the world make works of _____. It is also the reason why we _____. And since God created us, we have a responsibility to Him.

- **Genesis 1:28**

  God commands Adam, to be fruitful and _____. Since Adam and Eve were made in God's image, their children were intended to be in God's _____ as well.

God does not tempt anyone with evil.

- **Genesis 1:31**

  Everything that God created was very good including the first man and woman; there was no sin, wrong, or evil in them. The God of the Bible has never created anything that was not good.

- **Genesis 2:16,17**

  The first man and woman had the ability to love and obey God. But they were also _____ to choose to disobey God. God wanted them to freely choose to _____ Him. The condition was simple. God is a Holy God and must judge all sin. If they disobeyed God, _____ would be the result; _____ separation from God.

  As the man and the woman were faced with the choice of obedience or disobedience, notice that they had the following special gifts from God: They were made in the _____ and likeness of God. They were surrounded by a _____ environment. They had a constant, close relationship with _____. They had a true free choice, with power to obey or _____ to

SECTION A

disobey. The requirement was very simple, with both the command and the _____ clearly given.

- **Genesis 3:1-6**

    _____, in the form of a serpent, questions the Word of God and lies to Eve. Eve believes the lie of Satan and _____ God.

- **1st Timothy 2:13-14**

    Adam, though knowing it was a lie, also _____ God. Their spirits died immediately and their body and soul were corrupted by sin. They were separated from God, the only source of life. They became _____ because of their disobedience.

- **Genesis 3:7**

    By trying to cover themselves with the work of their own hands, they demonstrated that _____ had come upon them.

- **Genesis 3:23-24**

    Because of their sin they lost _____ with God and were put out of the Garden of Eden.

- **Romans 5:12**   Since Adam's fall, everyone who comes from Adam is born a _____.

- **Genesis 5:1-3**

    All who come from Adam and Eve are made in the image of Adam and not the image of God. Each time we look upon the body of one who has died, we should be reminded of the results of sin and that _____ are sinners.

- **1st John 1:10**

    Each of us has _____ sinned in the sight of God. We sin because we are born _____.

- **Isaiah 59:2**   You are _____ from God now because you are a sinner.

In summary, God made man. Man's body, soul and spirit were good. Man had a choice by which he could show his love for God through obedience. Man had a close relationship with God. He was in a perfect environment. Adam and Eve sinned. Since then, all people, including you and I, are born sinners and personally sin.

If appropriate, do the Reflect and Transfer on the next page.

Disciplers, when you see this icon, check the web site for guidance.

SECTION A

Reflect & Transfer

Take a moment to understand and learn so that you can share it.

What are the main points of this section? What part of this section stands out to you most? What questions do you have about this section? Are there parts of this section that you disagree with? How would you explain **1st John 5:7**? Are there any verses we want to memorize?

Here's a "water cooler" scenario: If your friend, over coffee, asks you "How could a loving God allow thousands of innocent people to be killed by terrorists or by disasters like tsunamis?" How would you respond to that question? *Need ideas? Visit www.TheJourneyForum.com.

Write **Romans 5:12** in the space below - going down a line at each punctuation mark.

_____

_____

_____

_____

_____

How would you explain that verse?

Salvation — Lesson 1

SECTION B

LESSON 1 — Salvation

The Saviour

Key Objective: To understand how God made a way back to Him.

- **Genesis 3:15**

As soon as the first man and woman sinned, God promised he would send a _____ through her "seed" meaning one who would be born. Even though Adam and Eve were guilty and deserved judgment, God, out of love, reached out to them (and to all of us) and gave the promise of a Saviour for mankind. But we are blind to our sin and even blind to our need of a Saviour. To make sure we know we are sinners and that we _____ a Saviour, God gave us the Ten Commandments.

The Ten Commandments are located in **Exodus 20:1-17** and here is a summary of them.

...Have no other gods before me... (God is to be first)
...Do not make graven images or idols . . . (including to make your own idea of God.)
...Do not take the name of the LORD ... God in vain...
...Remember the sabbath day, to keep it holy... (to worship God.)
...Honour your father and mother...
...Do not kill...
...Do not commit adultery... (even lust is adultery.)
...Do not steal...
...Do not bear false witness... (to lie)
...Do not covet...

Is there anyone who has not broken God's Law? God knows that men and women cannot keep His 10 Commandments. No one has ever kept the Ten Commandments or even had the right _____.

If someone asks you, "Don't you think all people are basically good?" How would you respond?

Romans 7:7

The Ten Commandments were not given to bring us to God or to remove our sin but to show us our need of a Saviour. God not only gave His Ten Commandments to help us, He also gave over 300 prophecies about the Saviour so that we would know who He is. To learn more about this, go to www.TheJourneyForum.com.

God knows we cannot save ourselves.

- But who is the Saviour? Read **Isaiah 7:14**

Immanuel means "God with us." The promised Saviour is _____ Himself!

Matthew 1:18-23 (This fulfills **Genesis 3:15** and **Isaiah 7:14**).

SECTION B

Let's now read a short summary of the teachings and life of the Saviour. What did the Saviour do and teach? We need to know who Jesus is from the Bible and who He said He is:

The passages below are from **Matthew** chapters **8, 16, 21; Mark 2, Luke 22; John 3, 19, Acts 1**.

While Jesus, the Son of God, lived on earth in the form of a man, He was tempted in all the same ways we are; yet He never sinned. He came to give His life for everyone. And, Jesus proved Himself as the promised Saviour in many ways. Jesus foretold that He must suffer many things, be rejected by the religious leaders, be killed, and then be raised from the dead on the third day.

Those suffering from different kinds of diseases were brought to Him, and He healed them all. He healed a man who had been lame for thirty-eight years. A man full of leprosy saw Jesus and fell on his face, saying, "**Lord, if you will, you can make me clean.**" Jesus then touched him, saying, "**I will: be...clean.**" Immediately the leprosy left the man.

While Jesus, the Son of God, lived on earth in the form of a man, He was tempted in all the same ways we are; yet He never sinned. He came to give His life for everyone. Jesus proved himself as the promised Saviour in many ways and Jesus foretold that He must suffer many things, be rejected by the religious leaders, be killed, and then be raised from the dead on the third day.

Jesus Christ said He could forgive sins...only God can do that. And Jesus had power over all spirits. Most of the religious and political leaders rejected Jesus' teaching. However, one called Nicodemus came to Jesus, and said "**We know that you...come from God: for no man can do these miracles... except God be with him.**" Jesus explained to him that God so loves everyone in the world that He gave his only begotten Son to die for us in our place, so that anyone who believes in Him will not perish and pay for their own sins, but have everlasting life. Nicodemus would soon understand and believe.

Jesus taught with great authority. He went into the temple and threw out those who were making profit in religion. Jesus said to them, "**It is written, My house shall be called the house of prayer; but you have made it a den of thieves.**" And Jesus taught, "**...what shall it profit a man, if he shall gain the whole world, and lose his own soul?**"

Jesus said, "**...I am the door: by me if any man enter in, he shall be saved,... I am the good shepherd: the good shepherd gives his life for the sheep...I give unto them eternal life; and they shall never perish...**"

Jesus said He is God.

Jesus offered hope over pain. He condemned sin but called the sinner to believe. He knew everyone's true thoughts and needs. He knows us the same way today. He offered then and now offers love, acceptance, belonging and a meaningful life now and eternal life with Him.

Jesus spoke with a woman at a well revealing that He knew everything about her, even the sinful acts in her life. He gave her hope for freedom from her empty life and she believed in Him and told everyone in her community about Him. Many believed because of her changed life.

Jesus spoke personally with an influential man who asked how he could inherit eternal life. Jesus invited the man to make an uncompromising commitment and follow Him, but the man went away sad.

After three years of teaching, Jesus knew His time had come to die for the sins of everyone. Jesus said to His disciples, "**Let not your heart be troubled:...In my Father's house are many mansions...I go**

SECTION B

to prepare a place for you...and I will come again, and receive you unto myself; that where I am, there you may be also..."

After the last supper, Judas came to Jesus with armed men from the religious leaders, greeting Him with a kiss of betrayal. Jesus knowing all things...said unto them, "**Whom do you seek?**" They answered him, "**Jesus of Nazareth.**" Jesus said, "**I am he.**" As soon as He said that, they went backward, and fell to the ground. Then Jesus allowed Himself to be tied up and brought to the religious leaders. He came for this purpose.

As soon as it was day, the religious leaders began to accuse Him before Pilate, the Roman ruler, saying, "**We found this fellow perverting the nation, and forbidding to give tribute to Caesar, saying that he himself is Christ a King.**" But Pilate said, "**I find no fault in this man...release him...**" And they cried out all at once, saying, "**Crucify him, crucify him...**" And Pilate said unto them the third time, "**Why, what evil has he done? I have found no cause of death in him...let him go.**" And they instantly yelled with loud voices, that he might be crucified. Then Pilate sentenced Him that it should be as they required.

Jesus paid the ultimate price for my sins on the cross.

Jesus was beaten and taken to a place called Calvary. There they nailed Jesus to the cross. He did this for you and me. Jesus prayed saying, "**Father, forgive them; for they know not what they do.**" After hours of suffering, Jesus, knowing that everything was now accomplished for His death, called out, "**It is finished.**" Then He bowed His head, and let His life go willingly.

Afterwards, two men took Jesus' body, wound it in linen grave clothes that were dipped in spices, and laid His body in a tomb. Then, as requested by the religious leaders, the tomb was sealed and guarded by Roman soldiers.

After three days, an angel of the Lord rolled back the stone from the tomb's door. In fright, the Roman soldiers fainted. When followers of Jesus came to the tomb and saw the stone moved, they were stunned. Suddenly, one of the angels said, "**Fear not...Jesus, which was crucified...He is not here: for he is risen, as he said.**" Then they remembered His words.

That evening, Jesus appeared to His disciples and said, "**Peace be unto you.**" He showed them the scars from the nails and the spear in His hands and His side. The disciples were filled with joy to see the Lord.

And Jesus instructed His disciples to go into the entire world and tell the Good News of Salvation because God loves us! His disciples gave their lives for Him because they saw Him alive.

The Resurrection proves Jesus Christ is God.

Jesus said to doubting Thomas, "**...because you have seen me, you have believed: blessed are they that have not seen, and yet have believed.**" Could that be you? Christ died for your sins...He was buried...and He rose again!

Jesus was seen by hundreds of people, showing them that He was alive. And He instructed His disciples,

SECTION B

"Go...into all the world, and preach the gospel (the good news of salvation)." As they watched, Jesus was taken up, and a cloud took Him out of their sight. Two angels said, "**this same Jesus, which is taken up from you into heaven, shall so come in like manner as you have seen him go into heaven.**"

- **John 20:30-31**

  Jesus Christ is God. Jesus was God before He was born to _____. He was God while He was on the earth. He proved He is God by His victory over sin and death and by His resurrection from the dead. And He is God _____ and He is alive now. He is the promised Saviour.

- **Matthew 20:28**   Jesus Christ came to give His life as a _____ to pay for our sins.

- **Romans 5:8**   He came to show us God's _____ even though we are sinners.

- **1st John 5:11,12**   He came to give us eternal life to _____ eternal death in Hell.

Salvation is trusting Christ alone.

1st Timothy 2:5

Notice that this verse says there is only one _____ between God and men. A mediator is one who restores peace between two parties. There are not several possible mediators; Jesus Christ is the only one because He is _____. He is the only possible intercessor between God the Father and man. He came to save you from your sins. Jesus Christ was either who He said He was or He was a liar. Jesus Christ could not just be a good teacher. He claimed to be God and He claimed to have the power to forgive sins. What do you believe?

Rejecting truth results in eternal separation from God.

- **John 3:18,36**

  God's _____ is clear. Because we are born sinners and we sin, we are already condemned and under the judgment of God. If we refuse the Son of God we _____ under the condemnation and judgment of God. God will not excuse any sin.

- **Revelation 20:15**   The Lake of Fire is God's punishment for _____.

- **Ephesians 2:8-9**

  Your religious works, your offerings, your church attendance, your baptism or any of your good deeds cannot change your sinful condition before God. No church and no religion can remove your sin. Only Jesus Christ can save you. Salvation is the gift of God. Salvation is never on the basis of any kind of _____ _____. The word "justified" means to be made right with God. Salvation is by faith plus nothing. You can do nothing to cleanse yourself from sin.

  Jesus Christ died and rose again to give you new life. Note: If you have already accepted Christ, then

SECTION B

let's review the joy of coming to Christ. If you are unsure about your salvation then go through this section carefully.

- **John 6:28-29**

Because of Jesus Christ, you now can come to God simply by _____, without works. Are you willing to _____ and trust by faith in the One True God for forgiveness of your sins?

- **Romans 6:23**

We deserve only one thing from God, and that is _____. God is completely holy and just and we deserve nothing but judgment. We have sinned. We have rebelled against God. But the last part of this verse says God has provided us with a way back to Him. It is not because God owes it to us; it is a _____ based on His love. The first man and woman were given a choice. However, they sinned and we also have sinned. We must all make a _____.

- **John 3:15-16**

God is standing with His arms open, telling us that even though we are all sinners, He has provided a way through which we may come to Him. God's promise is clear. If we _____ God's Son, the Jesus of the Bible, as our Lord and Saviour, then on the basis of Christ's finished work; His death, burial and resurrection as the only payment for our sin (which we trust by faith alone), God promises He will transfer us from the Kingdom of Satan to the Kingdom of God, from the family of Adam to the family of God, from a life of serving sin to a life of serving God, and from eternal death in Hell to eternal life in Heaven.

God promises you real life now and perfect peace, love, and joy with Him forever.

- **Romans 10:9, 10-13**

From our _____ we must believe that Jesus Christ is alive now and ask Jesus Christ to forgive us and save us. We trust Him only as our Lord and Saviour, by faith believing in Him alone as payment for our sins. You can pray now to put your complete trust in Jesus Christ as your Lord. For Jesus Christ to be your Lord means you surrender yourself, your will, your life, everything to Him. It means you will follow, worship and obey _____ Him.

Now God in His love has given you an _____ to be saved from your sins.

Would you like to surrender your life to Jesus Christ now?

I invite you to make this decision by asking God sincerely from your heart to save you. Here is a suggested prayer:

Lord Jesus, I confess that I am a sinner and that I need Your forgiveness. I am truly sorry for my sins and humbly ask You to forgive me and cleanse me. I believe that You died on the cross in my place and that You rose for my salvation. I surrender my will, my life, and my everything to You-- the Lord Jesus Christ. From this day forward I will follow and worship only You. You alone are my Lord and Saviour forever. By faith I accept from You the free gift of eternal life. I ask this in the Name of Jesus Christ. Amen.

SECTION B

Reflect & Transfer

Take a moment to understand and learn so that you can share it.

What are the main points of this section? What part of this section stands out to you most? What questions do you have about this section? Are there parts of this section that you disagree with? How would you explain **Romans 10:13**? Are there any verses we want to memorize?

Here's a "water cooler" scenario: If your neighbor asks you, "Why do you think Jesus is anything more than a good teacher?" Or "Why are Christians so intolerant to think that Jesus is the only way?" How would you respond?

Write **Romans 5:8** in the space below - going down a line at each punctuation mark.

_____
_____
_____
_____

How would you explain that verse?

LESSON 1: Salvation

Daily in the Word

Reading, Writing, Saying and Studying the Bible.

1. The Word of God, the Bible, brought you into salvation. Your attitude about God and His Word are so important, it will determine the direction of your life. It is important that you know the Bible is the very words of God and every word is pure. The Bible tells us the very thoughts of God. You can know your Heavenly Father by knowing His Word.

2. Read **1st Thessalonians 2:13**. If you received Christ, the Bible will work in you. And each word is important. The way to know God is through His Word.

3. Read **Hebrews 4:12**. You and I do not judge the Bible; it judges and knows us. We are to respect the Word of God and allow it to change us. You must obey the Word of God.

4. It is very important that you decide now to give time to God and His Word everyday. Our Lord Jesus said, in **John 8:31**, to those which believed on him, that if they would continue in His word, then they would be His disciples. And God's plan for your life is that you become His disciple. A disciple is a trained follower who places Christ first.

There are specific steps to discipleship in the Word of God and your discipler is with you to help you through each one successfully. You will learn how to meet with your Heavenly Father every day. If He is not leading you, your life will be too complicated.

All the problems and trials in life can be solved by our Heavenly Father. God is always at work and always moving. God wants to bring comfort and peace to your life even when you are in the middle of those troubles.

There is a spiritual struggle going on and you are on the winning side. Sometimes life is difficult because evil is fighting against God, but God will help you.

Online Resources

TheJourneyForum.com

There are many resources for Journey online. A few to check are:

1. 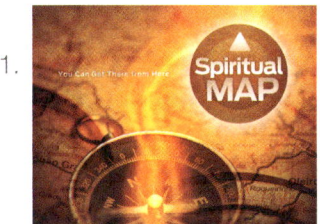 The Spiritual Map is a summary of lesson one to use as a witnessing tool.

2. Today, you might see a Hindu family across the street or Muslims in the stores or Buddhists in the airport. People from non-Christian beliefs are all around us and many are receptive to the Gospel. Are you prepared to share the truth of God's Word with genuine concern, drawing them to Christ?

There are tools to help you respond with the unique truths of biblical Christianity to point them to Jesus Christ, to answer questions, and win souls for eternity. Check the resources at www.TheJourneyForum.com regularly which include information on: Major Religions in our world, such as: Catholicism, Islam, Buddhism, Hinduism, Judaism. Major Cults in our world, such as: Jehovah Witnesses, Mormonism, Scientology, and others. Witnessing Tools like the Spiritual Map, Gospel Tracts, and more.

Go to www.TheJourneyForum.com and click on "Users."

Assignments for Lesson One

1. Get a note book with rings that you can put paper into. Then divide the paper with these sections: Daily in the Word, Prayer, Special Verses, Message Notes, and Bible Study. You need blank paper in each section.

2. Answer the questions for Lesson 1 below on a separate piece of paper and bring them to your next meeting:

   1. Which statement is true?
      a. God started evolution
      b. God created everything out of nothing
      c. God is in the trees, plants and wind

   2. Write out a Bible verse that teaches God is three in one.

   3. Does the Bible teach that Jesus Christ is God? _____. Write your reasons with Bible verses.

   4. Where did evil start?

   5. What does it mean that man was made in the image of God?

   6. What does it mean to be born in the image of Adam?

   7. Why is salvation not by our morality or religious good deeds or works?

   8. What do you believe about Jesus Christ?

   9. How do we receive salvation?

        Date completed : _____ Discipler signature: _____

SECTION A

The Word of God

Key Objective: To understand that I am safe and assured in God forever.

Because you accepted the Lord Jesus Christ as your Saviour, you are saved now and forever, and you can know it for certain.

- **1st John 5:13**

    From this verse, we can know for _____ that we have assurance of eternal life.

- Assurance of salvation means to know for _____ you belong to God, that you possess eternal salvation.

We can have a personal relationship with God.

- Your assurance of salvation is promised in the Bible. But before we look at those promises, we must understand more about the reliability of God's Word.

- The Bible is one of the oldest books in the world. The oldest parts are _____ years old. Even though the Bible is made up of _____ smaller books, it has one consistent message. The list of the books of the Bible is in the front of your Bible. Go to the table of contents in the front of your Bible any time you need to find a specific book until you can find them on your own. The Bible is divided into two sections: The _____ Testament and the _____ Testament.

- The Bible is often called the Word of God, the Holy Bible, or the Scriptures and is not like any other book. It's interesting to note that the Bible has always been the world's number one best seller since printing began.

- The Old Testament was originally written in the Hebrew language and the New Testament was originally written in the Greek language. The Bible has been translated into more languages than any other book in the world.

    Who is the author of the Bible?

- **1st Thessalonians 2:13**   The Bible says it is the _____ of _____.

- **2nd Peter 1:20-21**

    These verses teach three important facts: The Bible was not made by _____ ; godly men were used by God to pen the words; God is the _____ : notice it says "**...as they were moved by the Holy Ghost.**"

-  God used over 40 different men, over 1,500 years, from all different backgrounds to write down each word He wanted written. Most of the human writers God used to pen His words _____ knew each other. And yet the Bible completely agrees from beginning to end.

SECTION A

- It's amazing also that the Bible has never missed its predictions of thousands of events. Only God could be the author.

- **2nd Timothy 3:16-17**

  The way in which God gave us the Bible is called "inspiration". According to this verse, how much of the Bible is inspired? _____ _____.

God is the author of the Bible.

How can we learn and understand the Bible?

 1st Corinthians 2:9-13

The Holy Spirit teaches us the Bible when we _____ the words in the Bible to its own words. You must let the Bible define and speak for itself.

What did Jesus say about the Bible?

- **Matthew 5:17-18**

  The Bible would be fulfilled down to each _____ of a word and the smallest stroke of the pen.

- **Matthew 4:1-11**

  Jesus has all power, as God, and could have sent the Devil away at any time. But Jesus showed the importance and power of the Word of God by answering every temptation with the Word of God.

God's Word has enemies.

The Bible has enemies.

- Satan continually works against God and the Bible is one of his objectives. He has tried to ban, burn and remove the Bible throughout history. Countless Christian men and women have given their lives for the Word of God. You are holding a Bible in your hands right now because of their sacrifice.

- Even today, false teachers use translations to pervert the Word of God and, sadly, some have produced new Bibles for profit. We have to be careful that we know we have the Word of God. It's important for you to understand the position of our church on this issue (which we will provide for you).

- **Matthew 24:35**   His Words will not pass _____.

- **Psalms 12:6-7**   God promised to _____ His words forever.

- **Psalms 119:160**   Because the Bible is inspired of God, it is _____ from beginning to end.

SECTION A

- Your assurance of salvation is based upon the true Word of God. And you must always check every _____, teaching or _____ with the Word of God. This is why you must be Daily in the Word.

- In summary, based on what we have studied, the most important reason for you to believe in the final authority of the Word of God is that God wrote it.

- **Assignment:** Your Discipler will now explain and assign the "Daily in the Word" for Lesson Two, which is found toward the end of this lesson.

Reflect & Transfer
Take a moment to understand and learn so that you can share it.

What are the main points of this section? What part of this section stands out to you most? What questions do you have about this section? Are there parts of this section that you disagree with? How would you explain **2nd Peter 1:20-21**? Are there any verses we want to memorize?

Here's a "water cooler" scenario: If a friend at work says, "We can't really believe the Bible - it has too many contradictions" or "You Christians just believe everything you read in the Bible with blind faith" how would you respond? Need ideas? Visit www.TheJourneyForum.com.

Write **2nd Timothy 3:16-17** in the space below - going down a line at each punctuation mark.

_____
_____
_____
_____
_____
_____

How would you explain that verse?

SECTION B

Eternal Security

Key Objective: To know the promises of assurance in God's Word.

In this section we look at many of the specific promises in the Bible for assurance of salvation. Let's notice the "heart of God" in these verses and be comforted in his love for us.

- **John 3:16**   Your salvation is assured because God _____ you and me.

- **John 5:24**   I _____ everlasting life, I _____ _____ come into judgment.

- **John 6:37**   He will _____.

- **Acts 26:18**   I have _____ of sins.

- **Romans 5:1**   I have _____ with God.

The Bible holds promises for me.

- **Romans 6:23**   I have the gift of _____ _____.

- **Romans 10:13**   Those who call upon the name of the Lord shall be _____.

- **2nd Corinthians 5:21**   He has made me _____, meaning right with God.

- **Ephesians 1:6**   God _____ me in the beloved (meaning in Christ).

- **Ephesians 3:17**   Christ will _____ in my heart. Read **John 14:23**.

- **Colossians 1:14**   We have _____ through his blood.

- **Revelation 1:5**   He _____ me from my sins.

- **Revelation 21:27**   He recorded my name in the Lamb's _____ of _____.

In summary, we have learned that you can be assured of your salvation because of the reliability of God's Word and because of the specific promises of assurance.

Throughout Journey, we are not only learning biblical truths for every day life, we are also learning what it means to be a disciple of Jesus Christ. We do this by knowing and practicing the Steps of Discipleship.

Here is the first one to know:

The 1st Step of Discipleship: Become a Believer in Jesus Christ. **John 3:16**

There are a total of eight Steps of Discipleship found in God's Word.

SECTION B

Reflect & Transfer

Take a moment to understand and learn so that you can share it.

What are the main points of this section? What part of this section stands out to you most? What questions do you have about this section? Are there parts of this section that you disagree with? How would you explain **Romans 5:1**? Are there any verses we want to memorize?

Here's a "water cooler" scenario: A family member says to you, "How can anyone know for sure they are going to heaven?" What would you say? Need ideas? Visit www.TheJourneyForum.com.

Write **Romans 6:23** in the space below - going down a line at each punctuation mark.

_____

_____

_____

How would you explain that verse?

SECTION C

The Holy Spirit

Key Objective: To understand the Holy Spirit dwells in us.

We have seen that your assurance is based upon the reliability of the Word of God; we have seen the specific promises in God's Word about your salvation, and now we look at another way you know your salvation is sure:

One of the most important days of the year for Bible-believers is the day Jesus Christ rose from the dead. It is important because those who have trusted in Him will also be resurrected.

- **Romans 8:11**

The Resurrection is also important for another reason. After Jesus ascended up to heaven, He sent _____ _____ to live in all who receive Him as Saviour.

His Spirit lives in you now. That same Spirit of God that resurrected our Lord is alive in you to help you. God is in Heaven but He is also in union with you now and forever. God wants this truth to bring you an assurance of your salvation. Here are Scripture verses teaching that the Holy Spirit dwells in you:

- **Romans 8:9** The Holy Spirit comes to _____ in the believer.

- **Romans 8:16** God's Spirit _____ with our spirit that we are God's child.

- **1st John 5:10**

   I know I am saved because I have the _____ of the Spirit within.

   Can you ever lose your salvation?

- **John 5:24** says the kind of life you now have is _____.

- **John 10:28** says you shall _____ perish.

I have assurance because Christ dwells in me.

- **John 10:29** says no one _____ remove you from God's hand.

- **Romans 8:38-39** Nothing can _____ you from the love of God.

In summary, your assurance of salvation is based upon God's promises and His union with you. Visit www.TheJourneyForum.com to see more on this subject.

SECTION C

Reflect & Transfer
Take a moment to understand and learn so that you can share it.

What are the main points of this section? What part of this section stands out to you most? What questions do you have about this section? Are there parts of this section that you disagree with? How would you explain **Romans 8:9**? Are there any verses we want to memorize?

Here's a "water cooler" scenario: How would you answer this question, "Why are there so many religions if there is only one God?" And how would you respond if a friend says, "I don't feel saved, I think I lost it or never had it."

Write **Romans 8:16** in the space below - going down a line at each punctuation mark.

_____

_____

How would you explain that verse?

SECTION D

New Relationship

Key Objective: To understand our addition to the family of God.

We now see that our assurance of salvation is also based on the fact that we are God's children.

- **Romans 8:15**   God is your Heavenly _____.

- **Jeremiah 29:11-12**   God thinks about you and is deeply interested in your life.

- **2nd Corinthians 6:18** says those who trust Christ are the _____ and _____ of God.

- **Titus 1:2**   Your assurance of salvation is based upon faith in God who promised you forgiveness of sins and a relationship with Him. And God cannot _____.

My relationship with God is secure because He is now my Heavenly Father.

- It's important to know that you are in a spiritual struggle. Satan is doing all he can to work against God. Sometimes life will be hard because there is a battle going on for the souls of men and women. Sometimes the sin that is in the world will make life seem _____. But the power of Christ helps you each day. Jesus Christ died for you, but He also lives in you and you are in His family now.

  To meet the challenges you will face every day, it's very important for you to be Daily in the Word. Every day, reading, writing, and saying the Word of God also allows you to be obedient to John 8:31, where Christ told His followers that they would be His disciples if they were faithfully in His Word. This is a foundational step to becoming a disciple of Jesus Christ; to be in the Word of God every day.

  In conclusion, you have the Promises of God, through the perfect Word of God, the Spirit of God in you, and your new relationship with God to give you the assurance of your salvation. By accepting the Lord Jesus Christ as your Saviour, you are saved now and forever; and you can know it for certain.

SECTION D

Reflect & Transfer
Take a moment to understand and learn so that you can share it.

What are the main points of this section? What part of this section stands out to you most? What questions do you have about this section? Are there parts of this section that you disagree with? How would you explain **Romans 8:15**? Are there any verses we want to memorize?

Here's a "water cooler" scenario: A new Christian expresses doubts about his salvation to you. How would you explain assurance of salvation?

Here's another "water cooler" scenario: After witnessing to a family member and telling her about your salvation she says, "It's great that you've found something that works for you." How would you respond?

Write **2nd Corinthians 6:18** in the space below - going down a line at each punctuation mark.

_____

_____

_____

How would you explain that verse?

Daily in the Word

Reading, Writing, Saying and Studying the Bible.

Why write God's Word? Read **Deuteronomy 17:18-20** Look at the promises God made to the king over His people from writing the Word of God and following it: he would learn to fear the LORD his God, he would keep all the words of this law and these statutes, his heart would not be lifted up in pride, he would turn not aside from the commandments! As a result, he would enjoy success in life!

I believe God has these promises for you also, if you will be Daily in the Word. Kings are busy: plans to make, people to conquer, people to rule, assassinations to avoid, rebellions to put down, and a queen to keep happy. Busier certainly than most of us will ever be. But God commanded the King to hand write his own copy of God's Word. Why? God knew everyone would be watching the King. He was the leader. He was to be a role model. The King's subjects would follow his example. And God wants everyone to do this.

Another answer to the question of "Why write God's Word" is that something happens when you write out God's Holy Scripture that you can experience no other way; as you read the words you are about to write, and then say the words as you write them, sometimes you must glance back and forth to make sure you have the words letter-perfect. This slows you down to absorb and meditate on God's Word. Keeping the words in your mind long enough to say them and write them places the Word of God deeper in your heart.

Plus, there is the physical motion of writing. You are writing the Word of God, stroke-by-stroke, letter-by-letter, word-by-word, phrase-by-phrase, verse-by-verse. The very act of recording God's own words helps you see a truth you might otherwise miss.

Also, being Daily in the Word is a requirement for you to become a disciple. The first step you took was to trust in Christ for eternal life. The next step of discipleship is described in **John 8:31** where Christ told His followers that they would be His disciples if they were faithfully in His Word.

This step is foundational and vital for your Christian life. If you are Daily in the Word you will be obedient to Christ and mature spiritually to become, not just a believer, but a disciple of Jesus Christ. As you continue in Journey, each lesson will help you to become His disciple. So, here at the beginning, be faithful to do your Daily in the Word and you will be amazed at what God will do in your life.

1. Get alone and pray asking God to speak to you through His Word.

2. Find the section in the Bible assigned to you by your Discipler. Write the date and time at the top of the page of your Daily in the Word notebook.

3. Write the book, chapter and verse that you are starting to write on the next line in your notebook. Notice the words in the verses many times are divided by punctuation marks.

4. Now, read the words out loud up to the punctuation mark then write them on one line in your Daily in the Word notebook (and it's OK to say the words again as you write them).

LESSON 2: Assurance

5. Read the next part but write the words one line down in your notebook.

6. If you have a long verse that has no punctuation marks, divide it where you want to.

7. Write a minimum of 3 to 5 verses each day. Of course if you write more that's great. You are to do your Daily in the Word every day.

8. Do this every day and be ready to show your discipler your Daily in the Word Notebook the next time you meet.

Let's practice on **1st John 1:1-2**

_____
_____
_____
_____
_____
_____
_____
_____
_____
_____
_____
_____

 **Online Resources** TheJourneyForum.com

There are many resources for Journey online.

 Check The Assurance Guide which is a summary of Lesson 2 in Journey and you can use that with someone who has received Christ recently.

Assignments for Lesson Two

1. Your first assignment in being Daily in the Word, is to handwrite the book of 1st John. You can see a writing plan on the next page. Be sure to show your discipler what you have accomplished each time you meet. After you complete writing the book of 1st John, you may choose from several options which will be explained later. The important thing is for you to be obedient to Christ to continue in His Word.

This is the 2nd Step of Discipleship to know: a disciple is in the Word of God every day.

Join a tradition that God has used: think about this, until the printing press was invented, the only copies of the Bible were hand written. This went on for centuries. We have the Bible today because Christians wrote God's Word. Many, many Disciplers involved in Daily in the Word have finished their own copy of God's Word. Some, in other countries, have witnessed Bibles burned and banned and it means so much to them to write their own copy. Perhaps you would like to carry on this tradition that God has used to preserve His Word and write your own copy of the Word of God.

Remember, you are not just writing words. You are writing The Word. You will see the Truth...say the Truth... hear the Truth... remember the Truth and form the Truth in your heart as it flows from your pen onto paper.

2. Answer the questions for Lesson 2 below on a separate piece of paper and bring them to your next meeting:

   1. Answers to every problem in your life are provided by your _____.
   2. What is meant by "assurance of salvation"?
   3. What did you do to receive salvation?
   4. What three things is your assurance based upon?
   5. The Bible is made up of _____ smaller books.
   6. The Bible is divided into two sections: the _____ Testament and the _____ Testament.
   7. Explain what **2nd Peter 1:20-21** and **2nd Timothy 3:16** teach?
   8. How does Satan attack the Bible?
   9. Write a verse about the Bible being preserved.
   10. What is the most important reason to believe the Bible is our final authority?
   11. We must always check every _____, teaching or _____ with the Word of God.
   12. Write some of God's promises about your salvation.
   13. How can you learn the Bible?
   14. Write two things about the Holy Spirit and His work in your assurance of salvation.
   15. Can you ever lose your salvation? Why?

Date completed: _____ Discipler signature: _____

For more resources visit www.TheJourneyForum.com   Lesson 2 page 13

Journey
The Spiritual Formation of Multiplying Disciples.

Daily in the Word
Reading, Writing & Saying 1st John

LESSON 2 — Assurance

Daily in the Word

Reading, Writing, Saying and Studying the Bible.

Assignment: 1st John

The verses below are arranged by topics and/or stories. It's fine to write more than one group of verses per day. Some even write a chapter a day from the Bible. Take time every day to do your Daily in the Word.

Passage	Date	Passage	Date
1st John 1:1-2	_____	1st John 3:14-17	_____
1st John 1:3-4	_____	1st John 3:18-22	_____
1st John 1:5-7	_____	1st John 3:23-24	_____
1st John 1:8-10	_____	1st John 4:1-3	_____
1st John 2:1-2	_____	1st John 4:4-6	_____
1st John 2:3-6	_____	1st John 4:7-9	_____
1st John 2:7-11	_____	1st John 4:10-13	_____
1st John 2:12-14	_____	1st John 4:14-16	_____
1st John 2:15-17	_____	1st John 4:17-21	_____
1st John 2:18-19	_____	1st John 5:1-5	_____
1st John 2:20-25	_____	1st John 5:6-9	_____
1st John 2:26-29	_____	1st John 5:10-13	_____
1st John 3:1-3	_____	1st John 5:14-15	_____
1st John 3:4-7	_____	1st John 5:16-17	_____
1st John 3:8-10	_____	1st John 5:18-21	_____
1st John 3:11-13	_____		

Note to the Disciple: It rarely happens, but if you feel something is being taught that you are still not clear about, or if your Discipler will not meet with you regularly, please see your Pastor about this. Most of the time it is a misunderstanding and your Pastor can clear things up.

Prayer
LESSON 3

OVERCOMING SIN. HINDERANCES. LEARNING TO PRAY. EVERYDAY PRAYER. OUR FATHER, WHICH ART IN HEAVEN, HALLOWED BE THY NAME

SECTION A

Communication

Key Objective: To know my Heavenly Father through prayer.

Biblical Christianity is not just a set of beliefs, but a personal relationship to be enjoyed with God the Father, God the Son, and God the Holy Spirit. Simply put, we get to know someone by communicating with them. As a disciple and Discipler meet together around God's Word, they are to grow and experience biblical truths together. Each makes an impact on the other. In the same way, as we communicate with God and we grow closer to Him, we will come to know Him personally. The time we spend with the Lord in prayer is to be exciting and powerful. Now let's see what the Bible says about prayer.

- **Ephesians 2:18**

    Because of your salvation you can now communicate with your Heavenly Father.

- **Romans 10:13**

    Remember, He _____ you in answer to your prayer of salvation.

- **Jeremiah 32:17, 27**

    He is _____ _____. He can answer prayer.

- **Psalms 44:21, Matthew. 6:8**   He knows _____. He knows your needs.

True Christianity is a personal walk with God.

- **1st Corinthians 6:17**   He is _____ _____ you.

- **Philippians 4:6**   He wants to hear your _____.

- **Ephesians 3:20**   He can do _____ than you can imagine.

    Why should we pray?

- **John 16:24**   Prayer brings _____. God will help you with your problems.

- **Matthew 6:26, 10:29-31**   Pray because God is interested in the _____ details of your life.

- **1st John 5:14**   Pray because God will _____.

- **1st Peter 5:7**   Pray because God _____ about your troubles.

- **Jeremiah 33:3**   Pray because God _____ prayer.

SECTION A

- **Matthew 7:7-11**

  To summarize, God really cares about your communication with Him and He is concerned about the smallest details of your life. Now let's understand how we can communicate with God daily:

- **John 14:13**   Jesus said to "**ask in my name**". This means you pray what Jesus would pray.

- **Matthew 6:7**

  Do not use vain _____ (repeating words over and over). Vain means empty or worthless.

God hears my prayer and has the power to answer me.

- **Leviticus 26:1**

  The Bible commands us to not make _____. Many people around the world pray to idols. What are the idols in our culture?

- **1st Thessalonians 1:9**

  They turned to _____ from _____ to serve the living and true God.

- **1st Timothy 6:10**   Today, some trust in _____ and worship it or the things it can buy.

How Do I Pray?

- **Psalms 29:2**   Pray giving the Lord the _____ He deserves.

- **Psalms 32:5, 38:18**   Pray _____ and agreeing with God about our sin.

- **Psalms 62:8**   _____ in Him and _____ out your heart to Him.

- **Psalms 100:4**   Pray giving _____ to God.

- **Proverbs 8:17**   Love and _____ God.

- **Philippians 4:6**   Pray making specific _____.

- **Hebrews 4:16**   Come in prayer with confidence and you will find grace to help in time of need.

- **Psalms 119:18**

  Here is a simple plan for prayer: divide your time with God into these parts: begin with prayer asking the Lord to teach you, then Bible reading, then thinking about what God has said, then prayer again.

  When should you pray?

- **Luke 18:1**   _____, prayer is communication with God your Father.

SECTION A

- **John 6:23** Pray before each _____ giving thanks to God.

  Will my prayers be answered?

- **1st Thessalonians 5:17**

  We are to pray _____. This means that there is no time when we cannot communicate with our Heavenly Father. It also means we should never give up on the power of prayer.

- **1st John 5:14**

  Pray according to _____ _____, not our will. How do you know God's Will? His will is always in agreement with His Word. You will learn more about this in a coming lesson.

- **John 15:7** This is why Daily in the Word is important.

  Why is it required for us to have faith when we pray?

- Read **Hebrews 11:6** and **1st John 4:16**

  God is _____. God will always do to us and for us that which will ultimately be best for us. God's answers often seem delayed because He knows the best time for everything. God answers all our prayers, but not always the way we want or when we want. Our faith and trust in our loving Heavenly Father will help us to understand His answers. Our Heavenly Father is all-wise, all-powerful, and all-loving.

  This is the 3rd Step of Discipleship for us to know: A disciple is in prayer to God every day.

Reflect & Transfer

Take a moment to understand and learn so that you can share it.

What are the main points of this section? What part of this section stands out to you most? What questions do you have about this section? Are there parts of this section that you disagree with? How would you explain **1st Corinthians 6:17**? Are there any verses we want to memorize?

Here's a "water cooler" scenario: If your neighbor asks you, "What about those who never hear about Jesus? What will happen to them?" How would you respond?

Write **Ephesians 3:20** in the space below - going down a line at each punctuation mark.

_____

_____

_____

How would you explain that verse?

SECTION B

How to Pray

Key Objective: To understand how we can communicate with God daily.

In this section we will look at what is called the "Lord's Prayer" and obstacles to prayer.

Luke 11:1

To understand the context of the "Lord's Prayer" we must see that the disciples asked Jesus to teach them to pray. The Lord was not teaching them a prayer but rather how to pray. Jesus did not intend for this prayer to be prayed over and over because He said in **Matthew 6:7**, ...do not use vain repetitions.

The "Lord's Prayer" is found in several places in the Bible. We will look at it from **Matthew 6:9-13**.

- The "Lord's Prayer" is a _____ for prayer and teaches us many principles about prayer:

The words "**Our Father**" teach us the principle of our _____ with God.
The words "**in heaven**" teach us the principle of _____.
For His name to be "**hallowed**" teaches us the principle of _____.
For His "**kingdom**" to "**come**" teaches us the principle of focusing on _____ Kingdom.
For God's "**will**" to be done "**on earth, as it is in heaven**" teaches us the principle of _____ to _____ will.

The Lord's Prayer is a guide.

To ask God to give us "**our daily bread**" teaches us the principle of our _____ _____.
To ask God to "**forgive us our debts**" teaches us the principle of confession of _____.
The words "**as we forgive our debtors**" teaches the principle of removing _____ to prayer.
The phrase "**and lead us not into temptation, but deliver us from evil**" teaches us the principle of _____ and _____.
The words that it's God's "**kingdom, and the power, and the glory, for ever**" teaches us the principle of God's right to _____ in our lives.

We see that the "Lord's Prayer" teaches us how to pray. Now let's look at obstacles to prayer:

- **James 4:2**   An obstacle to daily prayer is just not _____.

- **James 4:3**   You ask with the wrong _____.

- **Proverbs 28:9**   An obstacle to prayer is failing to _____ to God's Word.

SECTION B

- **Psalms 66:18**

    Unconfessed _____ is an obstacle to prayer. Because communication with God is so important and vital to every part of your Christian life and because all of us deal with sin in our lives every day, we must understand how to deal with sin. As God's child, how does He view my sins?

- **Psalms 103:12** reads, As far as the east is from the west, Our sins, God will _____.

- **Hebrews 10:17** "And their sins and iniquities will I _____ no more." If all of my sins are forgiven, am I free to sin?

Sin hinders my relationship with Him.

- **Romans 6:1-2**   Shall we continue in sin? _____ _____. God says "NO!"

- **Romans 6:12**   Let not sin _____ in your body.

    Let's read the two main passages of Scripture, (**Galatians 5:19-21** and **Colossians 3:5, 8-9**) that deal with sins we commit in our world everyday. If you need to know the definition of some of the terms go to www.TheJourneyForum.com.

- **Hebrews 12:5-11**

    As a child of God, if you continue to sin God will discipline you as a _____ disciplines his children. But you will never lose your _____. A son or daughter can never stop being a son or daughter.

    Galatians 6:7-9   God will allow you to _____ according to what you sow.

    James 1:14-16   What is the final result of not dealing with sin? _____. As a Christian, your salvation is secure. But you can lose your peace, your joy, your closeness to God. Be in the Word of God everyday and be in prayer to God everyday.

    See Prayer Journals and other resources at TheJourneyForum.com.

SECTION B

Reflect & Transfer

Take a moment to understand and learn so that you can share it.

What are the main points of this section? What part of this section stands out to you most? What questions do you have about this section? Are there parts of this section that you disagree with? How would you explain **Matthew 6:7**? Are there any verses we want to memorize?

Here's a "water cooler" scenario: Your co-worker says to you, "I prayed for a promotion and I didn't get it. I thought prayer worked." How would you respond to them?

Write **James 4:2** in the space below - going down a line at each punctuation mark.

_____

_____

_____

How would you explain that verse?

SECTION C

Overcoming Sin

Key Objective: Understanding the obstacles to knowing God.

As a Christian, why do I still sin?

- **Ephesians 2:1-3**

  Understand that before you were saved, you walked according to the ways of this _____; you walked according to the _____ of the kingdom of the air; you fulfilled the _____ of your sinful nature and its desires and thoughts. (Lust means a desire for what is _____.)

- **2nd Corinthians 5:17**

  But the day you received Christ you were _____ . You received a new nature at your salvation but you still live in the world. You still have a very real enemy and you still have the same body and mind you had before you were saved.

- **James 1:14** The main source of temptation is our own _____ _____.

  How do I overcome sin today? Let's apply the following steps to a sin we are struggling with.

- **Psalms 119:9-11**

  _____ God's Word in your _____. This means that God's Word is internalized and affects your thinking, which in turn affects your behavior.

- **John 17:15-18**

  Everyday I must allow the _____ of God to _____ me from the world. Sanctify means to be set apart from sin to be used only for God's purposes.

My relationship with God grows with daily application of His Word.

- **1st John 2:12-14**

  I must allow the Word of God to _____ the enemy.

  Remember the 2nd Step of Discipleship: A disciple is in the Word of God everyday.

- Read **Romans 8:13, Romans 12:2, Colossians 3:5,16**

  I must allow the _____ of God to take the _____ of God to _____ (to drain of life) the deeds of my body and _____ my _____.

SECTION C

- **Psalms 119:59-60**

  How should you correct your life with the Word of God? _____

- **Luke 6:46**

  You must not only be Daily in the Word but you must also obey the Word so that your life style will reflect the teachings of God's Word.

  When disciples and Disciplers meet together it greatly helps with accountability. It encourages us not only to learn God's Word but to experience it; to put it into practice. As disciples mature spiritually, they are preparing to have their own disciple in the future.

  This is the 4th Step of Discipleship to know: A disciple and discipler meet together every week.

- Read **Proverbs 28:13**

  Now as God's child, you must accept _____ and acknowledge that you still sin. Your sin hinders your prayers and closeness to God. Through the prayer of salvation your sins are all forgiven. But now, as God's child, you admit your guilt for cleansing and to repent of the sin.

  Pray "I confess to the sin of _____ and _____ and etc". True repentance means you do not want to ever do that again. Go back and look at the list of sins from **Galatians 5** and **Colossians 3**. It is important that you look at the list. Go through them carefully asking God to reveal any areas of unconfessed sin in your life.

Communicating with Him helps me overcome the sin in my life.

- **Psalms 51:2**

  Lord, _____ me thoroughly from mine iniquity, and cleanse me from my sin.

1st John 1:9   If we confess our sins God will _____ us and cleanse us

Ask God in prayer to forgive and cleanse you. This is not for salvation but to break the power of sin you have allowed in your life, and to have a close relationship with your Heavenly Father. Stop now and pray for God to forgive you and cleanse you from each sin He has revealed to you. And each day ask God to help you.

Being a disciple of Jesus Christ means that you are taking out of your life those things that are not pleasing to God and adding to your life the things that are pleasing to Him. To help you continue to mature in your Christian life you need to establish these practices right away:

Do not allow sinful thoughts to control your mind.
Do not go to places or be with people that make it _____ to sin.
Be aware of the tactics of Satan that point you in the wrong direction (unforgiveness, bitterness etc.).

SECTION C

Be in the Word every day and actively communicate with God throughout each day.
Find those verses in God's Word that help you with your particular weaknesses or ask your Discipler to help find those verses.
Surround yourself with people who will encourage your walk with God.
View your Discipler as one with whom you can be totally honest to strengthen each other.

In conclusion, we have the incredible opportunity to know God through His Word and through communicating with Him. And He wants our lives to have peace and joy which comes from a life that is consistent with biblical truth.

Remember that throughout Journey, we are not only learning biblical truths for every day life, we are also learning what it means to be a disciple of Jesus Christ. We do this by knowing and practicing the Steps of Discipleship.

Let's review the steps we have learned so far:

1. Become a Believer by trusting in Jesus Christ as Savior from **John 3:16**.

2. A disciple is in the Word of God every day from **John 8:31**.

3. A disciple is in Prayer to God every day from **Luke 11:1**.

4. A disciple and discipler meet together every week from **John 13:33-35**.

There are a total of eight Steps of Discipleship to help us reach the Destinations of Spiritual Formation.

 **Reflect & Transfer** Take a moment to understand and learn so that you can share it.

What are the main points of this section? What part of this section stands out to you most?
What questions do you have about this section? Are there parts of this section that you disagree with?
How would you explain **Romans 12:1-2**? Are there any verses we want to memorize?

Here's a "water cooler" scenario: A person you work with asks you, "Why did my mother die from cancer?" How would you respond?

Write **John 8:31** in the space below - going down a line at each punctuation mark.

_____
_____
_____
_____

How would you explain that verse?

Daily in the Word
Reading, Writing, Saying and Studying the Bible.

Your Discipler will now take a thorough look at all the sections in your Daily in the Word notebook and give instructions if needed. Remember Christ told His followers that they would be His disciples if they were faithfully in His Word, John 8:31. If you are Daily in the Word you will mature spiritually.

Here are some additional ways to learn God's Word and to grow as a disciple:

Marking words. It's important that you continue to hand write God's Word and study His Word. As you are reading, saying and writing the words of God, some verses or words will just seem to jump off the page and capture your attention. These will be words that convict of sin, comfort, reveal sin, guide, give you peace and many other things. This is God's Spirit teaching you His Word. Underline those words, phrases and verses that get your attention. And write any questions, thoughts or notes in your Daily in the Word near those underlined words.

Notes from Messages. It's a great idea to take notes on the Bible messages you hear at your church and place them in the Message Notes section of your notebook. You are building God's Word in your life and placing it deeper in your heart.

Memory verses. Some verses and words will really touch your heart and life. Write those verses in the "Special Verses" section of your Daily in the Word notebook. Memorize and think about those verses from God's Word.

Prayer. It is very important to have regular times of prayer. Always begin and end the day with prayer. The truth is, every single one of us has a deep, inner need to know our Saviour. And prayer is not just going to your Father when you need something. Prayer is relating every area of your life to Him and His Kingdom for His Glory.

In prayer, God changes our will so that we conform to His Will. Prayer is the loving communication between you and your loving Heavenly Father. He longs to hear and answer the desires and needs of your life. Sometimes you need to pray until the "ache" in your soul stops hurting. Tell God exactly how you feel and what you fear. He saved you to have a close relationship with Him. God the Father is interested in every part of your life. God cares and loves you. Bring everything to Him - and then follow His leading.

Online Resources
TheJourneyForum.com

There are many resources for Journey online. Check the "Water Cooler Scenario" sections for help in preparing answers to real questions.

LESSON 3: Prayer

Assignments for Lesson Three

1. Now your assignment is to read, write and say the Gospel according to **Mark**. You should have finished writing 1st John in your Daily in the Word by now. Building God's Word in your life makes a permanent difference. This book was written by a disciple of Jesus Christ. Read, write and say at least 3 to 5 verses everyday. If you want to do more, that's awesome. You can see a writing plan on the following pages.

2. What should my prayer requests be? In order to grow in prayer, keep a list of prayer requests in the Prayer section of your notebook to see how God is working. Write the requests you have for others and yourself and write down the answers when they come. **Here is your assignment:** look up the verses below this week. Find the prayer request(s) in the verses. Bring your answers to your Discipler at the next meeting and use them as prayer requests in your prayer time:

2nd Chronicles 16:12	Psalms 119:18, 34, 133	Acts 4:29	James 1:5
Psalms 19:14	Matthew 5:44	Romans 15:30	James 5:14
Psalms 34:4	Matthew 6:11	Ephesians 6:19-20	1st Peter 5:7
Psalms 37:5	Matthew 9:37-38	2nd Thessalonians 3:1	
Psalms 51:2,10	Matthew 26:41	1st Timothy 2:1-4	

Date completed : _____ Discipler signature: _____

3. Begin to memorize all the Bible verses below. They are all verses that will help you witness and share the Gospel with others. Your goal is to know them by Lesson Nine. Quote or write new verses each time you meet with your Discipler and review what you have already learned.

Genesis 1:1	Genesis 2:16-17	John 10:28	John 3:36
Ephesians 2:4	Romans 5:12	Mark 8:36	Revelation 20:15
1st John 5:7	10 Commandments	Luke 5:20	John 20:31
Isaiah 14:12-15	John 11:43-44	Luke 7:48	Romans 10:13
Matthew 25:41	John 11:25-26	John 3:16	
Genesis 1:26-27	John 14:6	1st Cor. 15:3-6	

4. Answer the questions for Lesson 3 below on a separate piece of paper and bring them to your next meeting:

   A. What are some things we know about God from praying?
   B. Why should you pray?
   C. How should you pray?
   D. What does the Bible teach about idols?
   E. When should you pray?
   F. How will your prayers be answered?
   G. What is your plan for prayer?
   H. What does the Lord's Prayer teach you?
   I. What keeps your prayers from being answered?
   J. How does God see your sin after salvation?
   K. Why should you be in the Word of God everyday?
   L. Write the new Bible verses you are memorizing.

Date completed : _____ Discipler signature: _____

Daily in the Word
Reading, Writing & Saying the Gospel of Mark

Daily in the Word
Reading, Writing, Saying and Studying the Bible.

Assignment: The Gospel of Mark.

The verses below are arranged by topics and/or stories. It's fine to write more than one group of verses per day. Some even write a chapter a day from the Bible. Take time every day to do your Daily in the Word.

Date:	Date:	Date:
Mark 1:1-4	Mark 4:1-4	Mark 6:30-31
Mark 1:5-8	Mark 4:5-9	Mark 6:32-34
Mark 1:9-11	Mark 4:10-12	Mark 6:35-38
Mark 1:12-15	Mark 4:13-15	Mark 6:39-40
Mark 1:16-20	Mark 4:16-20	Mark 6:41-44
Mark 1:21-25	Mark 4:21-25	Mark 6:45-46
Mark 1:26-28	Mark 4:26-29	Mark 6:47-50
Mark 1:29-31	Mark 4:30-35	Mark 6:51-52
Mark 1:32-34	Mark 4:36-41	Mark 6:53-56
Mark 1:35-39		
Mark 1:40-42	Mark 5:1-4	Mark 7:1-4
Mark 1:43-45	Mark 5:5-9	Mark 7:5-8
	Mark 5:10-13	Mark 7:9-13
Mark 2:1-3	Mark 5:14-17	Mark 7:14-16
Mark 2:4-8	Mark 5:18-20	Mark 7:17-20
Mark 2:9-13	Mark 5:21-24	Mark 7:21-23
Mark 2:14-17	Mark 5:25-29	Mark 7:24-26
Mark 2:18-20	Mark 5:30-34	Mark 7:27-30
Mark 2:21-22	Mark 5:35-37	Mark 7:31-34
Mark 2:23-28	Mark 5:38-40	Mark 7:35-37
	Mark 5:41-43	
Mark 3:1-4		Mark 8:1-3
Mark 3:5-8	Mark 6:1-4	Mark 8:4-9
Mark 3:9-12	Mark 6:5-6	Mark 8:10-13
Mark 3:13-15	Mark 6:7-9	Mark 8:14-18
Mark 3:16-19	Mark 6:10-13	Mark 8:19-21
Mark 3:20-22	Mark 6:14-16	Mark 8:22-26
Mark 3:23-25	Mark 6:17-20	Mark 8:27-29
Mark 3:26-30	Mark 6:21-24	Mark 8:30-33
Mark 3:31-35	Mark 6:25-29	Mark 8:34-38

LESSON 3

Date: _____   Date: _____   Date: _____

Mark 9:1-3 _____   Mark 12:1-3 _____   Mark 14:41-42 _____
Mark 9:4-7 _____   Mark 12:4-8 _____   Mark 14:43-45 _____
Mark 9:8-10 _____   Mark 12:9-12 _____   Mark 14:46-47 _____
Mark 9:11-13 _____   Mark 12:13-17 _____   Mark 14:48-52 _____
Mark 9:14-18 _____   Mark 12:18-22 _____   Mark 14:53-55 _____
Mark 9:19-23 _____   Mark 12:23-27 _____   Mark 14:56-59 _____
Mark 9:24-27 _____   Mark 12:28-31 _____   Mark 14:60-62 _____
Mark 9:28-29 _____   Mark 12:32-34 _____   Mark 14:63-65 _____
Mark 9:30-32 _____   Mark 12:35-37 _____   Mark 14:66-68 _____
Mark 9:33-37 _____   Mark 12:38-40 _____   Mark 14:69-72 _____
Mark 9:38-41 _____   Mark 12:41-44 _____
Mark 9:42-46 _____   Mark 15:1-3 _____
Mark 9:47-50 _____   Mark 13:1-2 _____   Mark 15:4-6 _____
                                  Mark 13:3-6 _____   Mark 15:7-10 _____
Mark 10:1-5 _____   Mark 13:7-9 _____   Mark 15:11-14 _____
Mark 10:6-9 _____   Mark 13:10-13 _____   Mark 15:15-18 _____
Mark 10:10-12 _____   Mark 13:14-17 _____   Mark 15:19-22 _____
Mark 10:13-16 _____   Mark 13:18-20 _____   Mark 15:23-25 _____
Mark 10:17-18 _____   Mark 13:21-23 _____   Mark 15:26-28 _____
Mark 10:19-22 _____   Mark 13:24-27 _____   Mark 15:29-31 _____
Mark 10:23-27 _____   Mark 13:28-31 _____   Mark 15:32-35 _____
Mark 10:28-31 _____   Mark 13:32-34 _____   Mark 15:36-38 _____
Mark 10:32-34 _____   Mark 13:34-37 _____   Mark 15:39-41 _____
Mark 10:35-40 _____   Mark 15:42-44 _____
Mark 10:41-45 _____   Mark 14:1-2 _____   Mark 15:45-47 _____
Mark 10:46-48 _____   Mark 14:3-5 _____
Mark 10:49-52 _____   Mark 14:6-9 _____   Mark 16:1-4 _____
                                  Mark 14:10-11 _____   Mark 16:5-6 _____
Mark 11:1-4 _____   Mark 14:12-16 _____   Mark:16:7-8 _____
Mark 11:5-10 _____   Mark 14:17-21 _____   Mark 16:9-11 _____
Mark 11:11-14 _____   Mark 14:22-25 _____   Mark 16:12-13 _____
Mark 11:15-18 _____   Mark 14:26-28 _____   Mark 16:14-16 _____
Mark 11:19-21 _____   Mark 14:29-31 _____   Mark 16:17-18 _____
Mark 11:22-26 _____   Mark 14:32-34 _____   Mark 16:19-20 _____
Mark 11:27-31 _____   Mark 14:35-38 _____
Mark 11:32-33 _____   Mark 14:39-40 _____

Journey
The Spiritual Formation of Multiplying Disciples.

Local Church
LESSON 4

BOOK OF ACTS. BAPTISM. BIBLICAL LEADERSHIP. WOMEN IN THE CHURCH. FALSE TEACHERS. BIBLICAL COMMUNITY. REACH OUT. REACH I

SECTION A

The Local Church

Key Objective: To understand God's plan for the church.

In this section we see that God has a very specific plan for reaching out to a world of unreached people:

- **1st Corinthians 10:32**   In the Old Testament, God primarily worked through the _____ to get His Word to an unreached world. In the New Testament and in our time, God works through local _____ until His return to get His Word to lost Jews and Gentiles (a Gentile is anyone that is not a Jew). This verse lists those three groups.

- Notice in the table of contents of your Bible that seven letters in the New Testament are addressed to seven local churches **(Romans-Thessalonians)** and these letters contain the main body of _____ for New Testament Christians. Also, the books **1st and 2nd Timothy** and **Titus** are to pastors of local churches. And the book of Revelation addresses seven local churches. These simple observations clearly show that God is working through Bible-preaching churches and nothing can take the place of the church.

- God's plan is the multiplication of disciples through disciple-making local churches that teach and preach the _____ of _____.

Let's see how local churches developed after Jesus had finished training His disciples:

- **Acts 1:8**

    Before Jesus ascended into Heaven, promising He would return, He told His disciples to be _____ to the farthest places in the world.

- **Acts 2:41, 4:4, 5:14**

    After hearing powerful Bible messages in Jerusalem, _____ believe.

Through our church we reach our community and the rest of the world.

- **Acts 5:42, 6:1, 7**

    Notice that the disciples obeyed His command to care for and teach the new believers daily. The disciples multiply because they followed Christ's example and command. This illustrates the next step of discipleship for us to know: If you faithfully meet with your Discipler you will experience biblical truths for your life and your future disciples. When we are faithful to meet, the result will be _____.

- **Acts 8:1, 4**

    Persecution scattered the disciples from _____. The disciples who were scattered

SECTION A

proclaimed the _____ everywhere they went because they had been discipled.

- **Acts 9:31**

  Three years after the resurrection of Christ, _____ started in Judea, Galilee and Samaria and multiplied. This means that people became believers and they began to be discipled under the leadership of mature disciples forming a church in their location: a local church.

- **Acts 11:19-26**

  Eight years after the resurrection of Christ, a local church started in Antioch. This church is our _____ to follow. The Word of God will now focus on this church. A _____ number believed upon Christ in Antioch. So God brings leadership to the church and more _____ received the Lord in Antioch. Then the disciples were called _____ first in Antioch. Notice that there is a difference between being a Believer and being a Disciple.

God's plan today is the Local Church.

- **Acts 13:2, 14:23, 16:5**

  Three years later, in 44 A.D., the church at Antioch sent _____ who went and started churches. And those churches started other churches and so on. Biblical churches today are still following this strategic plan. True New Testament Bible-teaching churches started from our Lord's Disciples. These churches have made disciples and started other Bible-teaching churches since Christ's _____ disciples.

  Why are there so many churches and religions? We see in God's Word that Satan's strategy is to imitate and corrupt what God does. And the Bible records Satan's first attempt to organize false religion for his purposes at the Tower of Babel in 2200 B.C. Satan tried to work against God's plan of sending the Saviour through the Jewish people because he wants to be worshipped.

  Today God's plan is for the world to hear about the Saviour through Bible-believing churches. And it's not surprising that we see Satan establishing false churches to confuse people and work against God's church. That's why there are so many denominations. Satan is the author of false, man-made religions and false churches. Read **2nd Corinthians 11:3-4, 13-15**. Satan's main agenda is in religion

- What is a true New Testament Bible-Believing Local Church? It is a group of saved and discipled men and women who assemble together for worship and ministry with the leaders God has given them under the Word of God.

  What are the functions of a local church?

- **Acts 13:1-2**

  We are to _____ the good news of salvation at home and around the world.

- **Acts 18:8**   We are to observe the teaching of _____.

SECTION A

- **Romans 10:13-15** We are to _____ to send the Gospel globally.

- **1st Corinthians 11:23-27** We are to observe the _____ _____. (Explained at the end of this lesson)

- **Galatians 6:1** We are to restore sinful _____ to right living and service for Christ.

- **Ephesians 3:21** We are to bring _____ to God.

- **Ephesians 4:11-12** and **Ephesians 4:15** We are to mature disciples for _____.

- **Hebrews 10:25** We are to _____ together for worship and fellowship.

What is my responsibility to my local church?

- **Hebrews 13:17** _____

- **Ephesians 5:25** reads, Christ also _____ the _____, and _____ Himself for it; _____ your church. Pray for and love your Pastor. _____ your church. Financially send the Gospel to those in spiritual darkness through our local church. And we must be faithful to worship together and to serve in our church as directed by our Pastor. _____ discipleship. We see the importance and the great opportunity we have to make an impact for Christ through our local church. Now, let's understand the purpose of Biblical leadership in the church:

Ephesians 2:19-20, 4:11

Writing about the foundation of local churches, the Apostles (Christ's first disciples) and Prophets (men who spoke as God gave them the words to say) were in local churches until the Bible was completed around 90 A.D. Then they were not needed.

Today, there are _____ positions in local churches to be filled: "Evangelist" is the Bible word for what we call a _____. "Pastors" are the _____ of the local church. "Teachers" include _____.

- **Ephesians 4:12**

The Leaders are to equip, train or prepare _____. The work of the ministry is making _____. To edify is to _____ or build up. The purpose of the leadership of your church is to mature you for the work of the ministry. Ministry in the Bible always has these components: a person has the Word of God and they are transferring it to someone else. When someone is authorized by the leadership to disciple one on one, the entire purpose is to see people commit to Christ and build the Word of God in their life so they can do the same.

We have now learned Step #5 of Discipleship: A disciple is faithful in a biblical local church.

What are the qualifications for leadership in the church? For local churches to navigate through the challenges in our culture, we must be obedient to and strive for the qualifications that God gives us in His Word for leaders. The following two passages help us understand what a biblical pastor and leaders look like: Read **1st Timothy 3:1-7** and **Titus 1:5-9**.

SECTION A

Local Church LESSON 4

- Let's now take a look at the dynamic contribution of women in the church by seeing the ladies mentioned in **Romans 16:1-15**.

  Phoebe - She is called "our sister" meaning she is a _____. She was a _____ of the church which is at Cenchrea: She had been a _____ of many.

  Priscilla - She served the Lord with Aquila, her _____. They _____ their lives for the Lord. _____ the churches gave thanks for her. And they had a church in their _____.

  Mary - She helped them _____ for the Lord.

  Junia - She spent time in _____ with Paul for being a Christian.

  Tryphena, Tryphosa - These two ladies _____ for the Lord.

  Persis - Mother of Rufus - She labored _____ for the Lord and her _____ is serving the Lord. Julia and the Sister of Nereus - These two ladies _____ for others.

  Note: To know more about the amazing contribution women have made to Christianity, go to TheJourneyForum.com (click on Users).

- **Titus 2:3-5** Ladies, be encouraged to be a _____ of women.
  Why should we care about our local church? Because it's one of the institutions that God created for His work in our lives and the world. It is God's plan; it is God's design. God instructs us to assemble together, especially in the last days. (**Hebrews 10:25**) The most exciting life we can lead is in living for Christ and strengthening our church by multiplying Disciplers. Our involvement counts.

Reflect & Transfer
Take a moment to understand and learn so that you can share it.

What are the main points of this section? What part of this section stands out to you most? What questions do you have about this section? Are there parts of this section that you disagree with? How would you explain **Acts 5:42** and **6:1,7**? Are there any verses we want to memorize?

Here's a "water cooler" scenario: What would you say to invite a friend to your church and why they should visit?

Here's another one: A neighbor says "I don't think we should put the 10 Commandments on display because it breaks the wall of separation between church and state." How would you respond?

Write **Ephesians 5:25** in the space below - going down a line at each punctuation mark.

_____

_____

_____

_____

How would you explain that verse?

SECTION B

Be Baptized

Key Objective: To understand the importance of baptism.

The command of Christ was to go, make disciples and baptize them. So now let's look at some questions about Biblical baptism.

Can baptism save us or wash away our sins?

- Luke 23:39-43

The thief on the cross believed upon Jesus and Jesus said the man would be _____ _____ in paradise. The thief never was baptized, never joined a church, etc. He just _____. Salvation is by grace through _____ in Christ _____ _____ works.

When do we need to be baptized?

- **Acts 8:12** and **Acts 18:8**   Baptism always comes _____ salvation. This is why _____ cannot be Scripturally baptized.

Baptism is a testimony of my commitment to Christ.

What is the Biblical way to be baptized?

- **Matthew 3:16** reads, And Jesus, when he was baptized, went _____ _____ of the water:

- Acts 8:37-39

Because baptism is a picture of the death, burial, and resurrection of Jesus Christ, the Bible teaches baptism is by _____. To immerse is to be covered completely with water. No one in the Bible was ever baptized by someone sprinkling water on them. And the word "baptism" means to submerge underwater.

Why do we need to be baptized?

- Matthew 28:19-20

We are _____ to be baptized. And also, the act of going under the water and rising up is a _____ of what happened to the Christian believer:
  - **Romans 6:2-3**   He died - I died
  - **Romans 6:3-4**   He was buried - I was buried
  - **Romans 6:4-5**   He was raised - I have new life
  - **Ephesians 2:6**   He ascended - I ascended

- Water baptism is a picture of the _____ work God did when you received Christ. Also, baptism is a step of _____ for a disciple of Jesus Christ because baptism publicly testifies that Jesus Christ is your Lord.

SECTION B

Where should I be baptized?

- Baptism is a public testimony of your decision to trust Jesus as your Saviour and Lord. Because of this, believers need to be baptized by their local church.

  Have you been Biblically baptized?
  Take a moment with your Discipler and discuss if you have taken this step of obedience. If you have been Biblically baptized, share what that meant to you.

  Write the date or approximate date of your Salvation: _____
  Write the date or approximate date of your Baptism: _____
  Write the name of the Church which baptized you: _____

- Lord's Supper

  The topic of the Lord's Supper has more resources in the web site and at this point your church may have some information for you regarding this church service. As a general summary, the Lord's Supper, or the Last Supper, or Communion was the last meal Jesus shared with His Twelve Apostles before His death on the cross for all our sins. Since then, it has been an important act of our worship, led by your pastor for believers only. The bread, in the Lord's Supper, symbolizes the body of Christ that was "broken" for us. The 'cup' symbolizes His blood that washed away our sins forever. However, it is important to understand that the observance of the Lord's Supper does not help in any one's salvation.

  The purpose of the Lord's Supper is for self-examination and rededication of our lives to Christ. We do well to ask, "Are we living in a manner that shows appreciation for His sacrifice?" "Are we refusing to repent of any sin that was covered by His blood?" It is also a means for building fellowship with one another in the church, and serves to remind us of our future blessing in Him. Jesus told His disciples that He would eat with them again when His Father's kingdom is established. For more information, see your Pastor about this wonderful church service for Believers.

Reflect & Transfer
Take a moment to understand and learn so that you can share it.

What are the main points of this section? What part of this section stands out to you most? What questions do you have about this section? Are there parts of this section that you disagree with? How would you explain **Luke 23:42-43**? Are there any verses we want to memorize?

Here's a "water cooler" scenario: You have a young disciple and they ask you if baptism will wash away their sin. How would you respond?

Write **Matthew 28:19** in the space below - going down a line at each punctuation mark.

_____
_____
_____

How would you explain that verse?

SECTION B

Daily in the Word

Reading, Writing, Saying and Studying the Bible.

 Your Discipler will now take a thorough look at all the sections in your Daily in the Word notebook and give instructions if needed. Remember Christ told His followers that they would be His disciples if they were faithfully in His Word. **John 8:31**. If you are Daily in the Word you will mature spiritually.

Here are some additional ways to learn God's Word and to grow as a disciple:

Bible Reading Projects

There are times when you and your Discipler cannot meet together like during summer vacations or other reasons that keep you from meeting for a few weeks. The assignments below can be done together to encourage growth in God's Word. You also may feel the need for large amounts of the Word of God to be built into your life at times and these suggested projects can help you focus on specific goals.

Also, consider downloading and listening to God's Word on an iPod or similar device. Here are some choices:

- Old Testament
- New Testament
- Romans to 2nd Thessalonians
- Psalms 119
- Proverbs
- John
- 1st Timothy through Titus
- Genesis
- 1st and 2nd Peter
- Luke
- Exodus
- Joshua
- Judges

Let's review the steps we have learned so far:

1. Become a Believer by trusting Jesus Christ as Savior from **John 3:16**.

2. A disciple is in the Word of God every day from **John 8:31**.

3. A disciple is in prayer to God every day from **Luke 11:1**.

4. A disciple and discipler meet together every week from **John 13:33-35**.

5. A disciple is faithful in a biblical local church from **Ephesians 4:11-12**.

Lesson 4 page 8

Online Resources TheJourneyForum.com

If you have a smart phone or mobile device, you can download the lessons and other helpful materials directly to your device. Also, consider sharing with other disciples and disciplers how you are doing in your Daily in the Word. Go to TheJourneyForum.com and click on "Users." Remember to share the Spiritual Map every chance you can with someone who needs Christ.

Assignments for Lesson Four

1. Review any memory verses you have learned with your Discipler now.

2. Answer the questions for Lesson 4 below on a separate piece of paper and bring them to your next meeting:

    1. Explain **1st Corinthians 10:32**.
    2. Read **Acts 19:10** and explain how it was possible that all of Asia heard the Word of the Lord.
    3. Who started the first Bible-Believing Churches?
    4. What is a true New Testament Bible-Believing Church?
    5. What is the purpose of the Church Leadership?
    6. How should you regard the church leaders who follow the Word of God?
    7. What should you look for in a church?
    8. Explain what the Bible teaches about the role of ladies in the church.
    9. What is your responsibility to the Local Church?
    10. Explain why we need to be baptized.
    11. Give two examples of someone who was baptized after salvation. Support your answers with Scripture.
    12. What is the Biblical way to be baptized?
    13. (True or False) Baptism is necessary for salvation.
    14. Have you been baptized?
    15. Where and by whom?
    16. Write the new Bible verses you are memorizing now.

Date completed : _____ Discipler signature: _____

Note to the Disciple: It rarely happens, but if you feel something is being taught that you are still not clear about, or if your Discipler will not meet with you regularly, please see your Pastor about this. Most of the time it is a misunderstanding and your Pastor can clear things up.

MULTIPLIED. COST OF DISCIPLESHIP. STEPS TO MATURITY. ONE ON ONE. COMMITMENT. GOD'S STRATEGY TO SPREAD HIS TRUTH

Discipleship
LESSON 5

RODUCING. CHRIST MULTIPLIED. COMMITMENT. STEPS
MULTIPLIED. COST OF DISCIPLESHIP. STEPS TO MATURITY. STEWARDSHIP. COMMITMENT. GOD'S STRATEGY TO SPREAD HIS TRU
NE ON ONE. PERSONAL STE

SECTION A

Discipleship

Key Objective: To establish a biblical perspective of discipleship.

- Read **2nd Peter 3:9**. What is God's concern for all mankind? _____.

  _____ of people are in the world today. How is it possible for so many to hear the Good News of Salvation? God's plan is the same as His plan for the world to be _____: Reproduction. In other words, God's plan is _____.

  A disciple, by definition, is a trained follower of Jesus Christ, who draws others to Him and disciples them to do the same. In this lesson, we take a deeper look at the purpose of Biblical discipleship.

- **2nd Timothy 2:2**

  How did Timothy learn to serve God? _____ _____.
  What did Paul tell Timothy to do? _____ _____.

Multiplying disciple makers is God's strategy.

Let's review the steps of discipleship that you have learned so far:

- **John 3:16**

  Step #1 _____ in Jesus Christ as your Savior.

- **John 8:31**

  Step #2 A disciple is in the Word of God every day. If we are _____ in the Word, we will mature spiritually.

- **Luke 11:1**

  Step #3 A disciple is in prayer to God every day. If we communicate with God, we will know Him _____.

- **John 13:34-35**

  Step #4 A disciple and discipler _____ together every week.

- **Ephesians 4:11-12**

  Step #5 A disciple is faithful in a biblical local _____.

  There are three more steps to reach and in this lesson you will learn the next step of one on one discipleship:

SECTION A

- **Luke 14:33**

    Step # 6 is - A disciple is obedient to the Word of God and becomes a disciple maker.

    Jesus gave some specific requirements to be His disciple in Luke chapter fourteen. As we study this section consider the great call Christ is making to you personally to be His disciple.

- **Luke 14:26**

    Read **Matthew 10:37**.

    Jesus said He must come first in all your _____ for you to be His disciple. Consider the following question: Are you willing to be a disciple of Jesus Christ even if it appears it will cost you everything?

- **Luke 14:27**

    Jesus said He must come first in all your _____ for you to be His disciple. Consider the following question: Is there anything more important than my obedience to Christ?

- **Luke 14:33**

    Jesus said He must come first in _____; time, talents, finances, goals, desires, plans, affections-- in everything for you to be His disciple.

    The chart below pictures some of the major areas of our life. To be a biblical disciple of Christ, He must be first in every area. Discuss with your Discipler how well you are doing in each area.

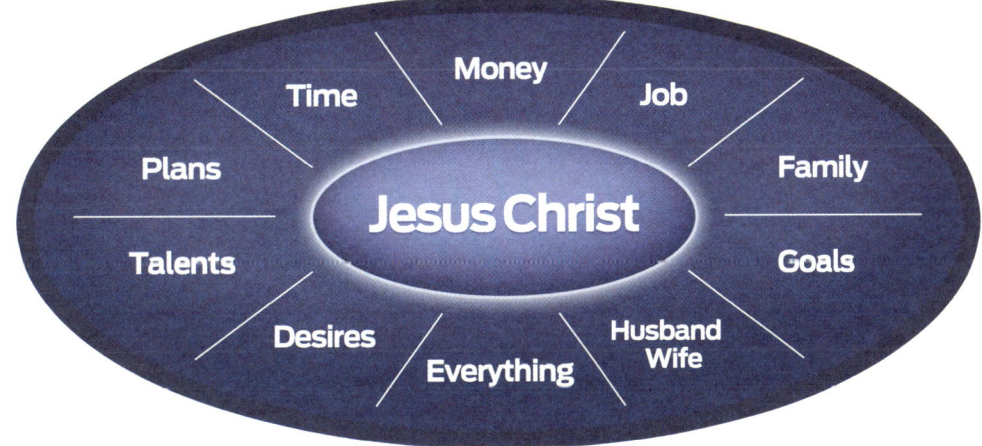

Some believers choose not to become a disciple because they think God may ask them to do something that they do not _____ to do, or because they think they know what is _____ for them instead of God knowing what is best, or because they are not sure that God has their best interests in mind, or for other reasons.

Read **Matthew 13:22** Jesus said that this person let the _____ of this world, and the deceitfulness of _____, choke the word of God in his life which produced _____.

SECTION A

- **John 6:66**

    Jesus had a large number of people following Him and some were not ready to take the next step. We have people in the church today like this as well. Jesus tested His disciples so He could focus on training those who would be faithful. He did this because He wanted the Gospel to reach around the world in every generation. Jesus requires faithfulness and He will test us today.

- **Matthew 6:25-33**

    Do you believe that God has a purpose for you? _____.
    Do you believe God knows what is best for you? _____.

    The Bible says you were saved for eternity by placing your faith in Christ. You can trust Him for each day also. Read **Jeremiah 29:11-12**.

A disciple is someone totally committed to Jesus Christ.

- **Luke 18:28-30**

    A man would not follow Christ but the disciples had _____ all and _____ Jesus. Jesus is teaching that the blessings of leaving all our own plans, dreams-- everything behind and following Him are far greater than any sacrifice we might experience.

    Remember that God has saved us from a life of hopelessness and eternal death to a life with purpose for eternity. Remember that He paid for our sins to bring us into His family. Remember that He loves us and has blessed us even though we are not worthy of it.

    To be a disciple of Christ, it is natural to respond to God our Father with "I will do whatever you want, whenever you want, wherever you want, to whoever you want by any means you want."

There are two decisions we want to consider now. The first decision deals with the direction and purpose of your life. The second decision deals with applying that first decision. The teachings of Christ in this lesson are all about being His disciple. He is calling for you to be His disciple today; not just a believer but a disciple by His definition.

The first decision to consider is, will you place Christ at the center, first place in your life in order to be a dedicated follower of Him? Second, will you complete your discipleship training to become a disciple maker?

This is a spiritual crossroad; we are talking about committing to becoming someone in Christ who has the characteristics of a mature disciple.

Now would be a good time to reflect on your journey so far, and ask yourself a question:

Do I want to be a committed disciple of Christ, and have I counted the cost? Stop now and quietly express to God in prayer what is in your heart.

SECTION A

Also, will you complete your discipleship training to become a disciple maker?

If you have accepted Christ's call for discipleship then inform your Pastor and make this a public decision as soon as possible in your church.

Reflect & Transfer
Take a moment to understand and learn so that you can share it.

What are the main points of this section? What part of this section stands out to you most? What questions do you have about this section? Are there parts of this section that you disagree with? How would you explain **Matthew 10:37**? Are there any verses we want to memorize?

Here's a "water cooler" scenario: Your neighbor wants to know what makes the Christian life so good; what would your answer be?

Write **Luke 14:33** in the space below - going down a line at each punctuation mark.

_____

_____

_____

_____

How would you explain that verse?

SECTION B

Stewardship

Key Objective: To learn how to be a good steward.

This part of the lesson is about stewardship in our lives and our great opportunity to partner with God using our time, talent and treasure. We will use the study of our treasure to teach us the Biblical principles.

First, it is important to remember that God made and owns everything.

- **Job 41:11** Everything under heaven is _____.

- **Acts 17:24-25**

  We are not _____, all ownership is with God. Everything belongs to Him; including everything we have.

  But God wants us to manage His possessions for Him. A manager or a _____ takes care of that which belongs to another. The Lord holds us accountable for taking care of the things He has given us like time, talents, skills, and resources.

- To see how God thinks, read **Matthew 25:14-28**.

Let's now look at one area of stewardship, which is giving. What are our reasons for giving?

- **Deuteronomy 8:17,18**

  We give because it is the Lord that gives us the ability to gain _____.

- **Matthew 6:19-21**

  We give because it is an investment in _____ riches and giving gets our eyes off riches that will fade away.

- **Matthew 6:24** We give because it makes us choose who we will serve.

I recognize that everything good is because of God.

- **John 3:16** We give because God gave Himself to save _____.

- **Romans 10:13-15**

  We give to save people from eternal _____ by spreading the Gospel.

- **1st Corinthians 6:19-20** We give because we are not our _____.

- **2nd Corinthians 8:8-9** We give to prove we are sincere in our _____ for Jesus Christ.

Lesson 5 page 6

SECTION B

- **2nd Corinthians 9:6**   We give because we reap what we _____.

- **Colossians 3:1-2**   We give because we are to seek those things which are _____.

- **Luke 14:33**   We give because Christ is _____ in our lives.

    Where am I to give financially?

- **1st Corinthians 16:2**

    You learned in the last lesson the importance and purpose of the local church. All giving in the _____ _____ is done in and through local churches that make disciples.

Being obedient in my giving promotes God's truth around the world.

What am I supposed to give?

You gave everything about you to Christ the moment you accepted Him as Saviour. _____ is His. That's what this lesson is all about. Your giving is to be out of a willing heart and because you love the Lord Jesus Christ.

Notice that the Bible way to give is in 4 levels:

- **Hebrews 7:8**

    A _____ is ten percent. The Bible teaches that giving ten percent of your earnings is a good beginning place of Christian obedience to God.

- **2nd Corinthians 9:7**

    This is _____ giving. As you grow in the Lord, you will go beyond the ten percent. You can be cheerful because God blesses giving.

- **1st Corinthians 16:2**

    This is _____ giving. This is giving according to the amount God has blessed you.

- **2nd Corinthians 8:2-3**

    This is _____ giving. When you give beyond your ability, by faith, God will work in ways you can not imagine.

For a disciple, true Biblical giving goes much further than giving money. It is turning over complete control of your life and resources to Jesus Christ; our time, talent, skills, resources, etc. When we give financially we are getting the Gospel to the unreached. If God has control of our lives, He will have control of all we have as well. The question now is, will you be obedient to expand the Word of God by giving

SECTION B

through your church? Yes ( )   No ( )

At what level or levels will you begin? Level 1 ( )   Level 2 ( )   Level 3 ( )   Level 4 ( )

When will you begin giving? _____

Note: make it a practice to use the giving envelopes provided at the church; put your name on it and your offering inside.

A growing disciple gives willingly out of obedience to His Word.

Notice: We have a certificate for you for making such great progress in Journey. Please email us at lesson5@thejourneyforum.com to inform us that you completed lesson 5. Thank you.

Lesson Five Approval:

Your Pastor's signature _____   Date _____

Your Discipler's signature _____   Date _____

Reflect & Transfer
Take a moment to understand and learn so that you can share it.

What are the main points of this section? What part of this section stands out to you most? What questions do you have about this section? Are there parts of this section that you disagree with? How would you explain **Colossians 3:1-2**? Are there any verses we want to memorize?

Here's a "water cooler" scenario: You have a young disciple who asks you if he is to tithe on his net income or his gross income. How would you respond?

Write **2nd Corinthians 9:7** in the space below - going down a line at each punctuation mark.

_____
_____
_____
_____

How would you explain that verse?

Daily in the Word

Reading, Writing, Saying and Studying the Bible.

Your discipler will now take a look at all the sections in your Daily in the Word notebook and give instructions if needed. Here are some more thoughts about studying the Bible:

Paragraph Study. Try doing your Daily in the Word by writing the verses between one paragraph marker to the next paragraph marker. Many times this is a complete thought.

Meditation. The words of the Bible are living words and the meanings, applications and blessings of each word are inexhaustible. To understand some things that God wants to teach, you will have to meditate on the Word of God. What is meditating on the Word of God? It is to quietly reflect on each word, it is to pray the words, it is applying the words in your daily actions.

How to meditate. There are many ways God may lead you to think upon His Word. Here are a few ideas, but develop your own. Memorize the words, such, **"Man shall not live by bread alone..."** and then quote the verse to the Lord as a personal prayer. For example, "O Lord, I am not to live by bread alone, but by every word that comes from You."

Repeat the verse several times, and each time emphasize a different word. For example, "**MAN shall not live by bread alone...**", "**man SHALL NOT live by bread alone...**", "**man shall not LIVE by bread alone...**"

Picture each word and its importance, and let the words grow in your heart, mind and soul by reviewing the Words that God has focused your attention on. Talk to God about His Words. Ask Him about His Words. Expect those Words to produce fruit in your life. Expect God to use His Words to help you make decisions and think correctly. "**...be transformed by the renewing of your mind...**" **Romans 12:2**. Ask God for truth. The Lord said "**If any of you lack wisdom, let him ask...**" Make sure you obey what God leads you to do.

Let's review the steps we have learned so far:

1. Become a Believer by trusting Jesus Christ as Savior from **John 3:16**.

2. A disciple is in the Word of God every day from **John 8:31**.

3. A disciple is in prayer to God every day from **Luke 11:1**.

4. A disciple and discipler meet together every week from **John 13:33-35**.

5. A disciple is faithful in a biblical local church from **Ephesians 4:11-12**.

6. A disciple is obedient to the Word of God and becomes a disciple maker from **Luke 14:33**.

Online Resources   TheJourneyForum.com

There are many resources for Journey online. Also, we have a certificate for you for making such great progress in Journey. **Please email us at lesson5@thejourneyforum.com** to inform us that you completed Lesson 5. We have a free download for you. Thank you.

Assignments for Lesson Five

1. With your Discipler, complete the Discipleship Training Module(s) on the following pages.

2. Answer the questions for Lesson 5 below on a separate piece of paper and bring them to your next meeting:

   1. Explain how we obey **2nd Timothy 2:2**.

   2. What is God's plan to get the Gospel all over the world?

   3. What is the cost of discipleship?

   4. Why did Jesus require believers to become disciples?

   5. What are the most important reasons for you to give offerings to the Lord?

   6. What are the 4 levels of giving?

   7. The Christian should give of his time, ministry and resources through the local church. Explain why this is true.

   8. Write the new Bible verses you are memorizing now.

   9. Write the six Steps of Discipleship you have learned so far with their Bible verses.

   10. Answer this **"water cooler"** scenario: A Christian says to you "Don't I have the right to do what I want with my own money?" What would you say?

   Date completed : _____   Discipler signature: _____

Discipleship Training
Module 1

Discipleship Training
Introduction and explanation.

- This is the first training module for Journey. Work on this with your Discipler.

- Seriously examine the content of these training modules. You need to know how to disciple but you also need a biblical philosophy of discipleship to last a lifetime.

- Anytime you need more resources or information, visit www.TheJourneyForum.com.

Module 1
The Definition of one on one discipleship.

- A disciple is a Believer who desires to _____ in the Word of God and Christ-like character by learning and _____ the Word of God.

- A discipler is a Believer who is regularly leading people to Christ and _____ them to do the same.

- Discipleship is leading a new, young or orphaned believer in the _____ of the Word of God and _____ to Christ so that he or she can win and _____ them.

- Discipleship involves developing a close friendship _____ with your disciple, teaching the Word of God, and _____ skills.

- Discipleship is the process by which a believer in the local church, with a _____ worth duplicating, commits himself or herself for an extended period of _____ to a teachable believer in order to guide their growth to spiritual _____.

- What is a concise definition of discipleship? Discipleship is Bible study; but it's not just that. It's a good relationship between the disciple and the discipler; but it's not just that. It's growing spiritually; but it's not just that. It's teaching the Bible; but it's not just that. It's accountability, training and evangelism; but it's not just those actions and certainly the list could go on and on. So what is a concise definition of Biblical one on one discipleship? It's multiplying soul winning disciplers for a lifetime.

Have your Discipler sign and date here when they review this assignment:

This assignment was completed successfully.

Date completed : _____ Discipler signature: _____

SECTION A

What's Next

Key Objective: To view the world from God's perspective.

The Word of God has many prophesies and has never missed any predictions. There are also many prophecies yet to be fulfilled. In fact, we are at a unique time in history called the "End Times" in the Bible. If we look around our world we see turmoil everywhere. We see the rise of false teachers, false religions, the assault against our culture and chaotic events in nature. All this has been prophesied in the Scriptures and the Bible clearly shows us what's next and how to succeed. The Bible puts the future in plain sight. And it's important to remember that the best is yet to come for us, in a truly wonderful life. But while we are here we must use every opportunity to spread the Gospel. Time is short. Let's see what the Word of God reveals about the future:

Ephesians 6:12

We are involved in a spiritual struggle and this verse identifies Satan's _____ army. More information about this verse is at www.TheJourneyForum.com

- **1st John 3:8**   Remember, the Enemy is already _____.

- **1st John 2:14**

   What makes you spiritually strong for these "End Times" difficulties? _____ _____.

We are involved in a spiritual struggle between good and evil.

- **1st John 4:4**

   Discuss these questions, from this verse: Who is in you?   Who is in the world?   Who is greater?

- **Ephesians 6:13-18**

   Notice what God has provided for us: loins girt about with truth, the breastplate of righteousness, your feet wear the Gospel, the shield of faith, and the helmet of salvation. These are weapons of _____.

   The other weapons or tools are the sword of the Spirit, which is the Word of God, praying always in the Spirit. These are weapons of _____.

- Compare the above to **Romans 13:12-14**.
   The Bible describes how this spiritual struggle will end and the end of this world - we don't know when the end will come, but we know it will be soon. The events below are described in detail in the book of Revelation. Let's see what God's Word teaches:

SECTION A

- First, know that a key event began "the final countdown" for our world in 1948 when the Jewish people went back to their homeland. This was prophesied thousands of years ago and it started God's final sequence of events.

The Bible tells us that this world will experience more chaos.

- **Matthew 24:3-8** and **2nd Timothy 3:1-4**

The Bible predicts that the world will become steadily worse. The complete description in the Bible tells of constant catastrophic events and a world that hates God. How do we see this happening today? But before the most terrible events take place, the Bible teaches we will be taken off the earth by Christ.

- Read **John 14:2-3, 1st Corinthians 15:51-52** and **1st Thessalonians 4:15-18**.

    Any moment now Christ will bring all _____ up to heaven. This is called the "_____". This word means "to be _____ up". Then we will forever be with the Lord. Our work on earth will be done.

    After the Rapture, the Bible teaches that seven years of Great _____ will take place on the earth. Tribulation means "time of trouble".

    This will be an awful time: death, disease, hunger, famine, earthquakes on a scale never seen before, entire seas contaminated, darkness, scorching of the earth by the sun, and many more judgments. The Bible teaches that two thirds of the world's population will die during the Tribulation.

- During this time a world leader will rise whom the Bible calls "The Antichrist." The Devil has his unholy trinity (the Devil, the Antichrist, and the False Prophet).

    The Antichrist will require everyone to receive a mark on their body. He will do many _____ by Satan's power and proclaim himself to be _____. The False Prophet will lead the world to worship the _____.

- During this time, two special _____ will be sent by God to turn people to Him (many Bible teachers believe these men will be Moses and Elijah).

    Also, God will choose and send 144,000 _____ missionaries during this time to go throughout the world with the Word of God.

- **2nd Thessalonians 1:7-9, 2:8-12**

    At the end of the Tribulation, the Antichrist and his forces make their final move to try and destroy the Jewish people. But at the last moment Jesus and His Heavenly army descend from Heaven and destroy the enemies of God. The Tribulation ends at this battle which takes place at _____ in the Middle East.

    Then the Devil will be bound for one thousand years. And Jesus Christ reigns as _____ over

SECTION A

the whole earth during that time. We call this "the Millennium" (meaning one thousand). The world will have the curse of sin removed from it and it will be like the Garden of Eden again.

- **Revelation 20:10-15**

At the end of the Millennium God will destroy the entire universe. Every person who did not accept Christ will stand before God and His Great White Throne to receive their final judgment. Satan will then receive his final punishment.

- **Revelation 21:4**

Then, finally, a new Heaven (Universe) and New Earth will be created which are perfect and beautiful. It's impossible to put into words how wonderful our life will be with God for eternity. His plan for all who believe is more than we can imagine or understand. As soon as you can, read **Revelation chapters 20 and 21** to see the description of what awaits you.

Christ is coming soon.

Here is a time chart picturing the events we just studied:

Visit www.TheJourneyForum.com to see more on this subject.

Important: Time is short. The sand is running out of the hourglass. At any moment Jesus will call us up to be with Him forever. The future belongs to disciples who are prepared not just to survive but to succeed in the "Last Days." The days ahead will become difficult and filled with distress. Be ready for what's coming. God said He would be with us until the end of the world. So don't go through the tough days ahead without staying close to Him and drawing as many to Him as possible.

SECTION A

Reflect & Transfer

Take a moment to understand and learn so that you can share it.

What are the main points of this section? What part of this section stands out to you most? What questions do you have about this section? Are there parts of this section that you disagree with? How would you explain **Ephesians 6:13-18**? Are there any verses we want to memorize?

Here's a "water cooler" scenario: A neighbor says to you, "There are so many religions in the world, how can anyone know which one is right?" What would you say?

Write **1st Thessalonians 4:17** in the space below - going down a line at each punctuation mark.

_____
_____
_____
_____
_____

How would you explain that verse?

SECTION B

The Judgement Seat

Key Objective: To know that we will give an account of our life.

The Word of God comforts us during these amazing but difficult "End times." Knowing how little time we have should encourage us to live for what is eternal and not for temporary values. To help us remember to use our time wisely, the Scriptures teach that all believers will give an account of their work for Christ. This event is called the _____ _____ of Christ. This may take place during the Tribulation in Heaven. Write this event on the chart on the previous page in its appropriate place.

I will be held accountable to God for how I lived.

- **Romans 14:10, 1st Corinthians 3:13-15** and **2nd Corinthians 5:10**

    At the Judgment Seat of Christ, all our works will be tested and revealed for what they really are. We may find that having the wrong motives for serving Christ will erase them. And nothing will be hidden. We can be sure that we will not lose our salvation but we will wish we could go back and change some things.

At the Judgement Seat of Christ there are 5 crowns that you can receive if you have earned them:

- **1st Corinthians 9:25**

    The _____ Crown is given for being a testimony for Christ to others. If we hurt the cause of Christ, we cannot receive this crown.

- **1st Thessalonians 2:19**

    The Crown of _____ is for those who draw people to Christ and multiply disciples.

- **2nd Timothy 4:8**

    The Crown of _____ is for those who keep in mind and love the appearing of the Lord Jesus Christ. If we live only for today or for ourselves, we cannot receive this crown.

- **James 1:12** and **Revelation 2:10**

    The Crown of _____ is for those who die for the cause of Christ and those who endure temptation. If we live a life full of sin, we cannot receive this crown.

- **1st Peter 5:4**

    The Crown of _____ is given to those who shepherd and lead others.

    At this Judgment, our _____ for Christ and our _____ will be judged. God always wants our hearts to be for Him. At this Judgment we will gain or suffer loss of reward. The rewards we receive at the Judgment Seat of Christ will be for eternity.

SECTION B

 1st John 2:28 and **1st John 3:2-3**

Because Christ is first in the life of a disciple and because Christ is coming any moment, we have to focus on eternal values. God works with us to reach the hearts and minds of those without Christ. And one day soon this struggle will be over and we can enjoy life eternal with our Saviour. But while we are here and while we still can, let's draw people to Christ and disciple them to reproducibility.

 **Reflect & Transfer** Take a moment to understand and learn so that you can share it.

What are the main points of this section? What part of this section stands out to you most? What questions do you have about this section? Are there parts of this section that you disagree with? How would you explain **Romans 14:10**? Are there any verses we want to memorize?

Here's a "water cooler" scenario: A family member tells you he's leaving his wife of 15 years to be with a man so he doesn't have to live a lie anymore. How do you respond?

Write **2nd Timothy 4:8** in the space below - going down a line at each punctuation mark.

_____
_____
_____
_____
_____
_____
_____

How would you explain that verse?

The Future — LESSON 6

Daily in the Word
Reading, Writing, Saying and Studying the Bible.

Your Discipler will now take a thorough look at all the sections in your Daily in the Word notebook and give instructions if needed. Remember Christ told His followers that they would be His disciples if they were faithfully in His Word. **John 8:31**. A disciple is in the Word of God every day.

Online Resources
TheJourneyForum.com

If you have a smart phone or mobile device, you can download the lessons and other helpful materials directly to your device. Also, consider sharing with other disciples and disciplers how you are doing in your Daily in the Word. Go to TheJourneyForum.com and click on "Users." Remember to share the Spiritual Map every chance you can with someone who needs Christ.

Reflect & Review
Take a moment to understand and learn so that you can share it.

Question	Struggling	Needs Improvement	Growing	Doing Well
How are you doing in your Daily in the Word?				
How are you doing in memorizing the Word of God?				
How are you doing in your daily prayer time?				
Are you faithfully meeting with your Discipler?				
Have you been water baptized Biblically?				
Are you faithful to attend and give to your Local Church?				
How are you at sharing the Gospel with others?				
What is your commitment level to one on one discipleship?				

Date completed : _____ Discipler signature: _____

Assignments for Lesson Six

1. With your Discipler, complete the Discipleship Training Module(s) on the following pages.

2. Pick 5 or more of the verses below and explain what they mean on a separate sheet of paper:

2nd Timothy 2:3	1st John 4:4
Ephesians 6:12	Ephesians 6:13-18
James 4:7	2nd Corinthians 5:10
1st John 2:14	1st Corinthians 3:13-15

3. Draw and label this chart on your own paper.

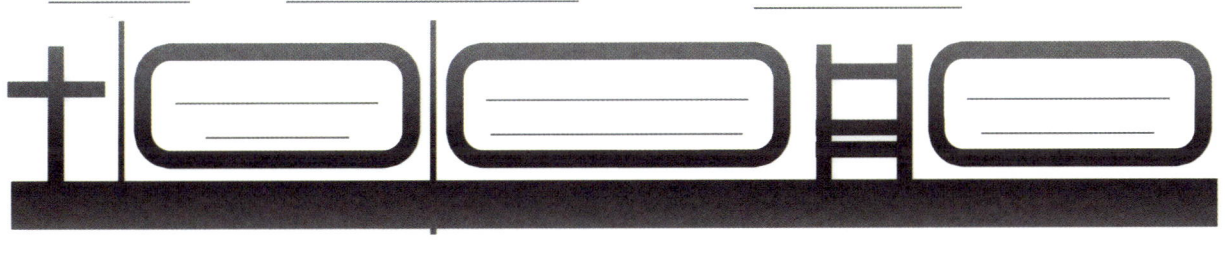

4. Memorize and quote or write the Steps of Discipleship as listed below at your next meeting.

   Step #1 Become a Believer by trusting Jesus Christ as Savior from **John 3:16**.
   Step #2 A disciple is in the Word of God every day from **John 8:31**.
   Step #3 A disciple is in prayer to God every day from **Luke 11:1**.
   Step #4 A disciple and discipler meet together every week from **John 13:33-35**.
   Step #5 A disciple is faithful in a biblical local church from **Ephesians 4:11-12**.
   Step #6 A disciple is obedient to the Word of God and becomes a disciple maker from **Luke 14:33**.

   Date completed : _____   Discipler signature: _____

Note to the disciple: It rarely happens, but if you feel something is being taught that you are still not clear about, or if your Discipler will not meet with you regularly, please see your Pastor for direction.

Discipleship Training

Module 2

Discover why discipleship is more effective one on one.

- Work on this with your Discipler.

- Adam and Eve were an _____ to us.

- Anyone can make _____ for one person.

- Discipleship helps the new believer when he or she is most vulnerable to _____ _____.

- Discipleship meets the new believer's individual needs rather than the _____ needs.

- Discipleship produces closeness, love and a deep _____ between the disciples.

- Discipleship provides the disciple with a friend to _____ ungodly friends.

- Discipleship provides the disciple with personal counsel to help make right _____.

- In Discipleship, exhortation, correction and admonition are _____ and easily done one to one.

- In Discipleship, the needs of the individual surface in the _____ of one to one meetings.

- It is interesting to note that in the Biblical steps of _____ you are instructed to go one to one.

- Not everyone can speak to a _____ but anyone can speak to one person.

- The life of the Discipler will _____ the truth of the Word of God. The disciple has a living example to follow.

- And most importantly, _____ had one main disciple. Notice some interesting facts about the one on one disciple of Jesus: _____ who is called "The disciple whom Jesus loved". Read **John 13:23, John 20:2, John 21:7, and John 21:20**.

    John was close to the _____ of Jesus. Read **John 13:23**.
    John knew that he would not _____ the Lord. Read **John 13:21-26**.
    John went all the way to the _____ with Jesus. He was the only disciple that did not run and hide or deny Christ. Read **John 18:15** and **John 19:25-27**.
    John _____ the Lord after the resurrection when others did not. Read **John 21:7**.
    John wrote about loving one another in the book of **1st John** -- the _____ disciple to do so.
    John received revelation about the _____ in writing the **Book of Revelation**.
    John was not _____ according to church history.

    Visit www.TheJourneyForum.com to see more on this subject.
    This assignment was completed successfully.

    Date completed : _____   Discipler signature: _____

SpiritualFormation
LESSON 7

STAGES OF SPIRITUAL GROWTH. MORAL PURITY. HUSBAND AND WIFE. PARENT CHILD RELATIONSHIPS. HOLINESS. THE STAGES OF SPIRITUAL GROWTH. MORA

SECTION A

How to be Holy

Key Objective: To understand the importance of purity.

This lesson is about purity and holiness in our day to day lives. There are many aspects of this subject but a few need to be addressed up-front: sexuality, drug and alcohol abuse. Our culture is displaying an ever bolder public promotion of sin with increasingly depraved practices. The media regularly promotes all of these areas and uses sexuality to advertise products visually. The world wants you to believe there are no penalties for violating God's law.

Our culture and Bible-believing churches are attacked with humanistic and secularist thinking daily. Even many Christians are influenced more in their concepts of love and morality by the media than by the Word of God. And with the rise of homosexuality, which is predicted in Scripture, we need God's guidance and power more than ever.

In God's Word, being enslaved to sin and sexual themes are discussed candidly. In fact, God created sexuality for important and good purposes. But God has limited it to marriage and has placed consequences upon disobedience of this standard. And God does not want us to be a slave to any sin in spite of the influences we see all around us.

In this lesson we want to look at why purity is important and a path to follow for victory.

- **1st Peter 1:15-16**

    First of all, God has called us to be holy. Our salvation is instant but our holiness is a _____ of growth. What is holiness or purity of life? It is living as Christ would live in motives, thoughts, words, actions, relationships, and making the right decisions morally.

    Why should we be holy? Certainly we want to avoid the _____ we see for sin but that shouldn't be the only reason. The whole concept of purity for the disciple is to be completely at God's disposal, ready for His use anytime, anywhere, and under any circumstance. Instead of a corrupt culture driving our life which leads to emptiness, we submit to God's way, committing to Him for a purposeful life that matters; a life that draws people to Christ and gives them real meaning for living.

Spiritual growth is a natural process.

A high "plane" of living for the disciple is to desire and to keep a nearness to God - to love God and to love an unbroken _____ with Him. We must view our relationship with God as something we foster. We must think that what we do and what we are is an opportunity to glorify Him. Being holy honors God and allows us to love Him with all our heart, mind and soul.

It also means having a desire to have purity within our human _____. If you are married that especially means purity to your wife or your husband. If you are single, it's your relationship to the guys or girls that you are involved with.

Also, being holy in our lives means we make decisions about what is right and wrong as a disciple of Jesus Christ.

SECTION A

Here is a simple set of "filters" to apply to decisions:
1. Is there a Bible principle that applies to this decision or action?
2. Is there a specific set of Bible verses about this?
3. Will this cause another Christian to be discouraged or weaker in their faith?
4. Is there Godly counsel available on this?

Take a minute and discuss with your Discipler how those questions would work on a particular decision.

Here are some important principles for holiness and purity in our lives:

- **Matthew 15:18**

The first principle to consider is that the problem starts inside us. Before we can have consistent purity in our lives, we must first admit and deal with the reality that impurity starts within. Pressures in our culture are huge but if we want to sin then it's really our _____ to temptation that is a root problem. Cleaning up our culture will not entirely solve the problem. The problem arises within our hearts.

- **1st Corinthians 10:12**

Here we see the most subtle of all errors; to think that we are somehow _____ and cannot be tempted. How many perceived public Christian leaders have we seen "fall" into sin? We must understand that a slow process within their hearts led to that end result.

- **John 17:15**

The second principle to consider is that our Lord prayed a specific prayer for our purity of life. Christ wants us in the world to be His "eyes," "mouth," and "hands" to an unreached world. He never wanted us in an isolated monastery or living in an Amish-type separation. He wants us in the world but He wants us _____ by the world's evil.

 John 17:16-17

Sanctify is a Bible word that means to be _____ for God's use alone. How do we achieve being in the world but not being worldly? It's by building God's Word daily in our lives.

- **John 17:18-20**

God wants me to live a principled life.

Just as Jesus came into a sinful world to do the Father's will, we are also sent into the world. We have a purpose for being here; not just to be holy and pure in and of itself, but to do what Jesus did while He was here. This prayer of Jesus was also for you and me. We are there in verse 20. Let us be encouraged to live a life separated from sin and separated to God's will for us.

- **2nd Corinthians 5:20**

Another principle is that we are in this world to _____ Christ. How we live reflects upon

SECTION A

Christ. When we go into the workplace or into our community, our life and lifestyle should represent Him properly. Discuss for a minute how ambassadors of our government relate to the foreign governments they are assigned to and how this applies to us.

- **James 4:7-8**

    We overcome Satan's attacks, not through direct conflict, but through _____ to God first, and second, through resistance to Satan's devices.

- **Romans 12:1**

    Another principle in having daily purity is to present ourselves to God; to _____ our lives to Him. This is a deliberate presentation of ourselves to God to be ready for His use anytime.

We are Ambassadors for Christ.

- **Romans 12:2**

    The world is trying to get us to think and live in its way, but we are not to conform to the moral system in the world. The opposite of holiness in our lives is living by the system that is in the world. "**Being transformed**" means a change that takes place on the inside. Living a pure life for God's use is dependent upon a _____ of our mental processes. This is one of the great benefits of discipleship; we are transforming our thoughts to God's way of thinking.

    How can I purify my life every day?

- **Psalms 119:9** and **1st John 1:9**

    Cleansing takes care of evil and affects how we live, act, and make decisions. How can we stay clean?

- **Psalms 119:11**

    Our holiness or purity of life will come from God changing us through His Word, not by us changing ourselves. Your attitude toward the Bible will greatly influence your daily _____ and ultimately your life. What is your attitude towards God's Word and your Daily in the Word?

- **Galatians 6:7**

    What are the consequences of immorality? We can see the consequences all around us: disease, suffering, premature death, loss of peace and joy in life, missing God's _____, and blessings, etc.

- **Romans 13:14**

    Don't make it easy to be unholy; make it hard. Remove the sources of temptation or remove yourself from the temptation. And being holy is not just a list of "don'ts." There are qualities God desires in our lives found in **Galatians 5:22-23** like love, joy, peace, longsuffering, kindness, goodness, faithfulness, gentleness, self-control as we become Christ-like.

Galatians 6:9

If you are single, are you willing to be single and biblically moral? If you are married, are you willing to be faithful in your marriage? A disciple of Christ is not a programmed person. Being a reproducible disciple of Christ is not what you do but who you are. It's your _____; your motivation. It's who you become. It's not only on Sunday, but a daily life from a holy perspective.

God does not demand that we live a life of sinless perfection in order to have fellowship with Him, but He does require, as disciples, that we be serious about holiness; that we confess and turn from the sin we commit, and that we desire to stay close to Him daily. Let's stop for just a moment and discuss the areas we are strong in and the areas of weakness we have.

If you desire, let's have a prayer of commitment, that from this day forward you are going to adopt God's definition for holy living and live that way.

 Below is a table that describes stages of spiritual growth commonly experienced. Sometimes we expect Christians to act spiritually mature when they are not. Sometimes we expect disciples to have a level of decision-making and purity of life when they still need to grow in Christ. As disciples grow spiritually, they gain a greater capacity to glorify God with their lives and to draw people to Christ. Now look at the stages of spiritual growth:

Stages	Characteristic	Problem	Need
Babe in Christ	Desires the Word	Unaware of spiritual truths	To be loved - assurance
Little child	Disobeys in word and actions	Easily deceived - weak	Protection and correction
Child	Little understanding	Complaining, gossiping	To be discipled
Young man	Strong in the Lord and has overcome the enemy	Many temptations and pride	To become a Disciple Maker
Father	Reproduces Disciplers	Priorities	Wisdom
Elder	Training Leaders	Victories and trials	Faithfulness
Aged	Leading Leaders	Transitions	Finish right

This chart is assembled from the following references: 1 Peter 2:2, Heb. 5:13-14, 1 John 2:1, 1 John 3:7, 1 Cor. 14:20, Eph. 5:8 1 John 2:14, Titus 2:6-8, Eph. 6:4, Col 3:21, 1 Cor. 4:15, 1 Peter 5:1, 1 Tim 5:9, Titus 2:2

Discuss these two questions: Where do you think you were on this chart when you started discipleship? Where do you think you are now on this chart?

SECTION A

Reflect & Transfer
Take a moment to understand and learn so that you can share it.

What are the main points of this section? What part of this section stands out to you most? What questions do you have about this section? Are there parts of this section that you disagree with? How would you explain **Romans 12:1-2**? Are there any verses we want to memorize?

Here's a "water cooler" scenario: A friend says to you, "I hope when I get married, it's for life. That's why I'm going to live together with someone first, just to make sure they're the right one before making that kind of commitment." Or a Christian says to you in passing, "Hey, they're not married, but it's working for them." How would you respond to these statements? After you make your comments to them, they say to you, "Judge not, lest ye be judged." What do you say then? Need ideas, visit www.TheJourneyForum.com

Write **Psalms 119:11** in the space below - going down a line at each punctuation mark.

_____

_____

_____

How would you explain that verse?

 # Daily in the Word
Reading, Writing, Saying and Studying the Bible.

 Your Discipler will now take a thorough look at all the sections in your Daily in the Word notebook and give instructions if needed. If you are Daily in the Word you will mature spiritually.

When you finish **Mark**, start on **Romans** to **2nd Thessalonians**. At The Journey Forum, there are other ideas for doing your Daily in the Word. You'll see other plans like these:

- Survey the Old Testament
- Survey the New Testament
- Survey the Life of Christ
- Read through the Bible in 30 days or 90 days.

Surveys are a combination of reading sections of the Bible, comparing Scripture and writing out key verses that you find.

More plans are being developed all the time that will help you with a life time of being in God's Word, so check the web site. The most important thing is that we put God first in our lives and we will if we are Daily in the Word.

 # Online Resources
TheJourneyForum.com

If you have a smart phone or mobile device, you can download the lessons and other helpful materials directly to your device. Also, consider sharing with other disciples and disciplers how you are doing in your Daily in the Word. Go to TheJourneyForum.com and click on "Users." Remember to share the Spiritual Map every chance you can with someone who needs Christ.

LESSON 7 — Spiritual Formation

Reflect & Review

Take a moment to understand and learn so that you can share it.

Question	Struggling	Needs Improvement	Growing	Doing Well
How are you doing in your Daily in the Word?				
How are you doing in memorizing the Word of God?				
How are you doing in your daily prayer time?				
Are you faithfully meeting with your Discipler?				
Have you been water baptized Biblically?				
Are you faithful to attend and give to your Local Church?				
How are you at sharing the Gospel with others?				
What is your commitment level to one on one discipleship?				

Date completed: _____ Discipler signature: _____

Assignments for Lesson Seven

1. With your Discipler, complete the Discipleship Training Module(s) on the following pages.

2. Download or read online the study on "How to Know God's Will" before your next meeting. If you have any questions, please write them down and discuss them with your Discipler. Look up each Bible verse in the study. (Go to www.TheJourneyForum.com and click on Users)

    Date completed: _____ Discipler signature: _____

3. Pick 6 or more of the verses below and explain what they mean on a separate sheet of paper:

    Romans 8:29 **1st Peter 2:11**

    Romans 12:1-2 **1st Corinthians 6:13-20**

    2nd Corinthians 10:3-5 **Hebrews 13:4**

    1st John 2:15-16 **1st Peter 3:1**

    1st Corinthians 7:1 **2nd Peter 3:18**

    1st Thessalonians 4:3-7

    Date completed: _____ Discipler signature: _____

Module 3

Procedures for one on one discipleship.

* * Work on this with your Discipler.

- Take time to talk and _____ to your disciple at each meeting.

- There are times you will not even _____ the lessons. But always encourage your disciple with the Word of God.

- The disciple is not to complete the lessons _____ on their own.

- In some cases, the Discipler is to only give one _____ of the Journey lessons at a time as the Discipler and disciple are meeting and studying together.

- The lessons are to be _____ by the Discipler. Do not assign pages of a Journey lesson _____ of the meeting.

- Never _____ a Bible verse in the lessons. Have your disciple _____ each verse.

- _____ your Daily in the Word notebooks.

- When you start each lesson read any introduction to them and _____ what you have already learned.

- Look up every _____ verse on each page in the lessons with your disciple.

- _____ the verses and the lesson.

- Teach the _____ of each key word in the Bible verses that are studied in the lesson.

- Do not assign the _____ at the end of the lessons until you have completed teaching the lesson.

- Do not go on to the _____ lesson until you have completed an evaluation of your disciple (the evaluations are in the lessons) and been given permission by the church leadership.

- _____ what you have learned when it is time to stop.

- At the _____ of each meeting ask, "What are you going to do about what you have learned today?"

- Close with _____. Schedule your next appointment. Record your meeting in your records.

- Remember: To _____ for your disciple.
  How you disciple them will determine how they _____.
  Then remember to get your disciple _____.
  Journey is only one to one and begins with _____.

Have your Discipler sign and date here when they review this assignment:
This assignment was completed successfully.

Date completed : _____ Discipler signature: _____

Module 4
The Value of one on one discipleship.

* Work on this with your Discipler. Jesus spent three and a half years teaching His disciples so that when He was _____, they would disciple others. This was His only _____ to reach the whole world in every generation to follow.

- The value of one on one discipleship to a disciple:
  Discipleship protects the disciple from _____.
  Discipleship gives the disciple loving, gentle _____.
  Discipleship _____ the disciple.
  Discipleship provides the disciple with a personal _____ to replace the ungodly friends.
  Discipleship teaches the disciple godly _____.
  Discipleship provides the disciple with counsel to help make right _____.
  Discipleship stops _____ behavior.
  Discipleship increases the disciples' _____ rate.

- The value of one on one discipleship to the Discipler:
  Discipleship prevents _____ in the disciple.
  Discipleship purifies the Disciplers' _____.
  Discipleship teaches the disciple how to _____ his or her disciple from the Word of God.
  Discipleship develops ministry _____ in the Discipler.
  Discipleship teaches the Discipler how to _____ another believer into a ministry.
  Discipleship brings _____ to the Discipler when the disciple grows in Christ: **3rd John 4**
  Discipleship teaches the Discipler how to inspire and _____ others to serve Christ.
  Discipleship _____ the Discipler as he or she ministers the Word of God.
  Discipleship teaches the Discipler how to preach or _____ the Word of God.
  Discipleship teaches the Discipler how to _____ the Word of God.
  Discipleship helps the Discipler to pass on what he or she has _____.
  Discipleship keeps the Discipler _____ about their Christian service.

- The value of one on one discipleship to the local church:
  Discipleship increases the number _____.
  Discipleship gets everyone working towards a common _____.
  Discipleship stops the church from _____.
  Discipleship finds _____ people and puts them in the spotlight.
  Discipleship brings more _____ to Christ.
  Discipleship strengthens your local church by developing godly _____.
  Discipleship strengthens the church _____.
  Discipleship increases the number of people being personally _____ for.
  Discipleship causes new churches to _____ naturally.
  Discipleship most importantly allows the church to be _____ to Christ.

- The value of one on one discipleship to the world:
  Discipleship is the _____ plan Christ gave out of love for the whole world. Discipleship is the only way the whole world can hear the Gospel and not _____. Discipleship will make it possible for Disciplers to go to other _____ to make disciples.

  Visit www.TheJourneyForum.com to see more on this subject.

  Have your Discipler sign and date here when they review this assignment:
  This assignment was completed successfully.

  Date completed : _____   Discipler signature: _____

FAITH, THE HOLY SPIRIT, WHAT IS FAITH? CHALLENGES AND SUFFERING, HEROES OF TEH FAITH

Faith
LESSON 8

WHAT IS FAITH? CHALLENGES AND SUFFERING, HEROES OF TEH FAITH, THE HOLY SPIRIT, WHAT IS FAITH? CHALLENGES AND SUFFERING, HEROES OF TEH FAITH? CHALLENGES AND SU

Faith

Key Objective: To understand how to have faith.

This lesson teaches what the Bible says about faith. Biblical faith means having _____, _____ or _____ in God and His Word. It means you stop trusting _____ and trust Him. It means _____ dependence on God. Faith releases you from your limited _____ to His unlimited, all-powerful abilities.

What is Faith?

- **Hebrews 11:1**

  Faith has _____. Faith has _____. We can see the results of living by faith and we can see tangible evidence that living by faith is real.

- **Hebrews 11:6**

  Without _____ it is impossible to _____ God. God can be trusted and He will _____ those who trust Him and live by faith.

- **Ephesians 2:8,9**   We are saved by grace through _____.

- **Galatians 5:22**   Faith is evidence we are being _____ by the Holy Spirit.

- **2nd Corinthians 4:18**

  The things we see are short-lived; the things we do not see are _____.

I must trust God every day.

- **Romans 10:17**   Biblical faith comes by hearing the _____ of _____.

- **Matthew 6:25-34**

  Faith _____ worry, false emotions and doubt.

  Have faith in God. If we have our faith in the one true God of the Bible, then we should know these facts:

- **Numbers 23:19**   God keeps His _____.

- **1st Chronicles 28:20**   God _____ fail.

- **Job 42:2**   God knows _____.

- **Malachi 3:6**   God cannot _____ from what He is. He will always be full of love for you.

SECTION A

- **Matthew 24:35**   You can _____ God's Word.

- **Titus 1:2**   God cannot _____.

   Faith during Trials and Suffering:

   James 1:2-4 and 1st Peter 1:7

   The Bible also teaches our faith will be _____. These trials can _____ our faith.

- **John 16:33, 2nd Timothy 3:12**

   Disciples will _____ trials of different kinds. Remember that you joined in a _____ for the hearts, minds and souls of all people the day you received the Lord. We will all have times of _____ and trials and hardships. In fact, there may be times when we will suffer just because we are _____ of Jesus Christ. But we can still experience the love and peace and joy that Jesus Christ came to bring.

- **Deuteronomy 31:8**   God will never _____ you during suffering and trials.

- **Matthew 5:11-12**

   Those who suffer for Christ's sake will receive a great _____ in Heaven.

- **2nd Corinthians 4:8-18, 1st Peter 4:19**

   When we suffer we should _____ Christ and continue to live a _____ life.

God never promised my life would be free of trials.

- **1st Peter 3:13-17**

   When you suffer, ask yourself, "Am I suffering for doing right or doing _____?"

- **1st Peter 4:1-2**   Trials cause us to stop the _____ in our life and to do God's Will.

- **1st Peter 4:12-19**   Discuss what you think this means.

- **Romans 12:19**

   God cares for us when we are suffering, but He does not want us to take _____ on those who cause us suffering. He will do what is just and right with those who persecute His _____.

- **Romans 8:28**

   We can be comforted in knowing God works everything for _____ to those who love Him.

SECTION A

- **Matthew 7:7-11**

    Pray for specific help in time of need and trial. _____ God's help and answer by faith.

- **Isaiah 45:5-6** and **Isaiah 46:9-10**

    Remember your faith is to be in _____. Biblical faith is always a decision to _____

    God and this decision leads to Biblical _____.

God provides me strength and faith through difficult times.

Examples of those who have lived by Faith:

Your Discipler will now assign you to read this week in the Old Testament about the Heroes of Faith listed in **Hebrews 11**. Look at the act of faith that is listed in **Hebrews 11** for each person, then find it in their story, and underline it in your Bible: Abel in **Genesis 4**, Enoch in **Genesis 5**, Noah in **Genesis 6**, Abraham in **Genesis 12**, Sarah in **Genesis 17**, Isaac in **Genesis 27**, Jacob in **Genesis 48**, Joseph in **Genesis 50**, Moses in **Exodus 2**, Israel and the Red Sea in **Exodus 14**, Joshua and the battle of Jericho in **Joshua 6**, Rahab in **Joshua 6**, Gideon in **Judges 6-8**, Barak in **Judges 4-5**, Samson in **Judges 13-16**, Jepthah in **Judges 11-12**, David in **1st Samuel 16-30**, Samuel in **1st Samuel 1-3**.

Date completed: _____ Discipler signature: _____

- **Ephesians 5:20** and **1st Thessalonians 5:18**

    In summary, a disciple of Jesus Christ lives by faith and trusts in God, not only for salvation, but in all areas of _____. How does God want us to respond to every situation? We must be _____ dependent on God, which is faith in action. In problems, trials and suffering, make the _____ to rely on His power and faithfulness. Also in great challenges and accomplishments, only trust God to lead you. God will then give you His grace and His power and you will know your Heavenly Father in a deeper, _____ way.

    Visit www.TheJourneyForum.com to see more on this subject.

SECTION A

Faith — LESSON 8

Reflect & Transfer

Take a moment to understand and learn so that you can share it.

What are the main points of this section? What part of this section stands out to you most? What questions do you have about this section? Are there parts of this section that you disagree with? How would you explain **Hebrews 11:1,6**? Are there any verses we want to memorize?

Here's a "water cooler" scenario: Your disciple says to you, "I feel God is calling me to be a missionary. What should I do now?" How would you counsel them?

Write **1st Thessalonians 5:18** in the space below - going down a line at each punctuation mark.

_____
_____
_____

How would you explain that verse?

For more resources visit www.TheJourneyForum.com

Daily in the Word
Reading, Writing, Saying and Studying the Bible.

Your Discipler will now take a thorough look at all the sections in your Daily in the Word notebook and give instructions if needed. If you are Daily in the Word you will mature spiritually.

When you finish Mark, start on **Romans** to **2nd Thessalonians**. At The Journey Forum, there are other ideas for doing your Daily in the Word.

Online Resources
TheJourneyForum.com

If you have a smartphone, you can download the lessons and other helpful material directly to your device.

Also, consider sharing with other disciples and disciplers how you are doing in your Daily in the Word. See The Journey Forum for more details.

Reflect & Review
Take a moment to understand and learn so that you can share it.

Question	Struggling	Needs Improvement	Growing	Doing Well
How are you doing in your Daily in the Word?				
How are you doing in memorizing the Word of God?				
How are you doing in your daily prayer time?				
Are you faithfully meeting with your Discipler?				
Have you been water baptized Biblically?				
Are you faithful to attend and give to your Local Church?				
How are you at sharing the Gospel with others?				
What is your commitment level to one on one discipleship?				
Are you preparing to have your own disciple?				

Mark the memory verses you have learned so far:

- ( ) Genesis 1:1
- ( ) Ephesians 2:4
- ( ) 1st John 5:7
- ( ) Isaiah 14:12-15
- ( ) Matthew 25:41
- ( ) Genesis 1:26-27
- ( ) Genesis 2:16-17
- ( ) Romans 5:12
- ( ) 10 Commandments
- ( ) John 11:43-44
- ( ) John 11:25-26
- ( ) John 14:6
- ( ) John 10:28
- ( ) Mark 8:36
- ( ) Luke 5:20
- ( ) Luke 7:48
- ( ) John 3:16
- ( ) 1st Cor. 15:3-6
- ( ) John 3:36
- ( ) Revelation 20:15
- ( ) John 20:31
- ( ) Romans 10:13

Assignments for Lesson Eight

1. With your Discipler, complete the Discipleship Training Module(s) on the following pages.

2. Write the Steps of Discipleship you have learned and pick 7 or more of the verses below and explain what they mean:

Hebrews 11:1	Hebrews 11:6	Romans 10:17	Ephesians 2:8-9	2 Cor. 5:7
James 1:2-4	1st Peter 1:7	John 16:33	2nd Tim. 3:12	Deut. 31:8
Romans 12:19	Romans 8:28	Isaiah 45:5-6	Isaiah 46:9-10	1st Peter 4:1-2

   Date completed : _____ Discipler signature: _____

   Write your answer to this **"water cooler" scenario:** How would you counsel a Christian who says to you, "My father died painfully from cancer and I feel angry that God would allow that."

3. Complete the study on the Holy Spirit before your next meeting with your discipler. Write your answers on a separate sheet of paper.

   As you work through this lesson, carefully study the ministry of the Holy Spirit, so you can understand His part in your life. The Holy Spirit's ministry in your life is rich and full, bringing joy into your life as you walk in His power.

   God has given us three resources to produce growth in our Christian life and walk. First, He gave the Word of God, which lays out the guidelines by which we should live. Second, He gave the people of God so we could be discipled. Third, He gave the Spirit of God to empower us in our walk as a disciple.

   The Holy Spirit's ministry in our life as believers is of utmost importance.

Explore truth about the Holy Spirit and how He affects our life.

1. Read **John 16:5-14**. Jesus is teaching His disciples about the Holy Spirit and His ministry. Having read this passage, consider the following questions:
   a. When would the Holy Spirit's ministry begin in the life of these men?
   b. According to verses 8-11, what is His ministry to the people of the world?
2. From verse 13, what were some of His ministries to these disciples?
3. Would the Holy Spirit glorify Himself or Christ?
4. According to **John 14:16-17**, when the Holy Spirit would come where would He dwell?
5. **Acts 1:4-8** are Christ's final words to His disciples prior to His ascension. Answer these questions from these verses:
   a. What would the Holy Spirit give these men?
   b. What would the Holy Spirit's power enable them to do?
6. As Christ concluded His earthly ministry, He paved the way for the Holy Spirit's coming. Pentecost, found in **Acts 2**, is the event when the Holy Spirit made His appearance. Since that day, the ministry of the Holy Spirit is unique and exciting.

7. The Holy Spirit is, first of all, a person. From the following passages we will see He possesses and performs those activities which only people who possess personality can do.
8. Look up the following verses and jot down the activities which the Holy Spirit performs:
   a. **John:14:26**, b. **Acts 13:2**, c. **1st Corinthians 2:10**.
9. From these verses write down some of the ways the Holy Spirit is affected as a person:
   a. **Acts 7:51**, b. **Ephesians 4:30**, c. **1st Thessalonians 5:19**.
10. In the following verses consider some names of the Holy Spirit and describe how His name is used in connection with other persons. a. **Genesis 1:2** b. **John 14:16** c. **John 14:17** d. **Romans 8:9**
    From these passages we can conclude that the Holy Spirit is a person. Personality means He possesses will (the ability to choose), intellect (the ability to reason and think), and emotion (the ability to feel). The Holy Spirit does not have a physical body as we have, but He does have personality.
11. Read the Scriptures that reveal some of the activities that He performs as God.
    a. **Genesis 1:2** b. **John 16:8-11** c. **Titus 3:5** d. **2nd Peter 1:21**
13. Who is the Holy Spirit? He is God, and as God He is one of the persons that make up the triune God. He is also a person with whom we can have a personal relationship.
14. Now, let's turn our attention to the work that the Holy Spirit performs in the life of every Christian. Some of these works happen immediately at salvation, and some are ongoing continually in our life. Consider the ministries the Holy Spirit performed when you trusted Christ for salvation.
    a. The indwelling of the Spirit: Read **John 14:17** – the promise of it. Read **1st Corinthians 6:19,20** - the reality of it. Read **1st Corinthians 3:16-17** and explain what responsibilities you have since the Holy Spirit indwells your physical body.
    b. The sealing of the Spirit: Read **Ephesians 1:13-14**. According to verse 13, what is God's seal upon your life, indicating you belong to Him? Verse 14 teaches that you are sealed until when?
    c. According to **Romans 8:16**, what does the Spirit do?
    d. What do **Romans 8:26-27** teach about the Holy Spirit?
    e. Look up **Ephesians 5:18**. What command is given in relation to the Holy Spirit?

    According to this verse, what controls a person when he is drunk? Obviously, God does not want you controlled by alcohol. What is supposed to control your life?

CONCLUSION
1. Look up **Galatians 5:16-25**. According to verses 16 and 17, what are the two conflicting natures in your life?

2. Verses 22-23 give the qualities the Holy Spirit wants to produce in you. List them:
   When the Holy Spirit is in control, these are the qualities present. To be filled with the Holy Spirit is to yield our life to His control. This should be our desire and request each day . . . to live out today under the influence and control of the Holy Spirit. It is the Holy Spirit who empowers us to be able to live victoriously in our walk as a Christian.

   Attempting to live victoriously apart from the power of the Holy Spirit is impossible. The only way to live your Christian life is by the power of the Holy Spirit. You ask, "How am I to be filled?" Look up **Luke 11:13**. The Book of James says we have not because we ask not. We need to surrender to God and ask God to fill us each day with His Holy Spirit to enable us to live victoriously.

   Date completed : _____ Discipler signature:_____

Module 5
Accepting a disciple and becoming a good communicator.

* Work on this with your Discipler.

    One on one discipleship involves spiritual _____ and demands a _____ commitment.

    One on one discipleship is not designed to just be a "nice" Christian activity but rather to change _____.

    Remember, the lessons are only _____ to reach the _____ of Discipleship. Be available for God to take you _____ He has disciples to be made. Be faithful when you are _____ because one on one discipleship will bring testing. One on one discipleship demands _____ to God in our daily lives.

- Before accepting a Disciple:

    Plan before you meet, but _____ on the Holy Spirit to lead you. Before accepting a disciple ask yourself: what can I remove from my life and _____ that takes away from one on one discipleship?

    Ask yourself: "Does _____ want me to accept this relationship?" "Am I willing to accept this responsibility?" "Is my _____ at a place where I can do this?" "Has the _____ led that person to be my disciple?"

    Count the _____ before you commit yourself to a life of one on one discipleship. When you accept the _____ of a disciple, follow through on your _____.

- How to be a good communicator with your disciple:

    Have other _____ Bible verses ready. Explain the lesson with _____ and personal _____.
    Do not go too _____ through the lessons and do not go too _____.
    Remember it is not the _____ but the Word of God.
    Never _____ them what you can show them or what you can _____ them.
    Remember this may be _____ to your disciple, and the concepts will be new.
    Use words that are _____ to your disciple and explain unfamiliar words.
    _____ the lesson ahead of the meeting and know the lesson.
    _____ the Word of God in the lessons thoroughly.
    Know the _____ and the _____ of each lesson.
    Have the lessons and their subjects listed in order in the _____ of your _____ so you know where you have come from and where you are going.

    Have the _____ of Discipleship in the front of your notebook and _____ refer to them.

    Visit www.TheJourneyForum.com to see more on this subject.

    Have your Discipler sign and date here when they review this assignment:
    This assignment was completed successfully.

    Date completed : _____ Discipler signature: _____

Module 6

Getting started with your new disciple.

Understand that pure one on one discipleship is leading an _____ person to Christ and teaching them to observe all things Jesus commanded.

Remember, one on one discipleship is _____ one to one. Meet with your disciple every week.

Men should only meet with men and women with women. Close _____ members should not disciple each other whenever possible (there can be exceptions in extreme circumstances).

Do not use the lessons that you disciple with as Sunday school lessons, sermons or for any other _____ than one on one discipleship.

One on one discipleship is the only way to reach the world and is the one reason we are left on earth after our salvation. Some or all of your disciples should be people you have _____ to Christ.

If a new or young disciple leads someone to Christ _____ the disciple has completed one on one discipleship, they may disciple the new believer with Lesson One and Two of Journey. But the disciple must complete Journey and receive _____ to disciple from the church leadership.

Do not go on to the next _____ if the disciple is not obedient or does not completely understand.

All assignments are _____.

Try to get your disciple through the entire _____.

Inform your church _____ of any unusual situations.

The way you _____ a one on one discipleship relationship may determine its _____.

Be excited, encouraging and loving in all your _____.

Try to disciple in such a way that you would want your disciple to disciple your _____ when they are old enough.

You will find that in one on one discipleship there are two _____ and two _____ at the same time. When we teach we _____, when we disciple we are _____.

Never assume the disciple is a _____. Be ready to go over the Spiritual Map with them and confirm their _____. You must get their story of how they came to know the Lord as Saviour.

You must immediately establish that God's Word is the _____ for this relationship.

The disciple is to be discipling before they _____ from the final lesson.

- Here are some of the main points of your first meeting with your disciple:

    Let us begin with _____. Our purpose in meeting together is:

    To _____ spiritually together.

Lesson 8 page 11

To develop you into a _____; not just to complete lessons.
And not to finish but to reproduce other _____.

We must keep our conversations _____ unless something is life threatening or very, very serious.

If I do not know the answer to a question you have, I will study and _____ an answer or ask you to wait because the question is answered in coming _____.

We can continue meeting together if both of us are _____ to the Word of God. The Word of God is our final authority and guide. The Word of God is so important for our lives. We cannot grow spiritually without it. If you disagree with any of the teaching, please let me know.

I want you to know that there will be _____. We will help each other to be faithful.

- Ask your disciple to answer the following questions. This may not be needed for new believers.

  When did you receive the Lord? How did you come to know the Lord? What were you like before you were saved? What were the circumstances of you getting saved? What changed in your life after you were saved? Where did you attend church before? Are you new to the Bible? Would you say you believe the Bible is God's Word? Why? How did you come to this church?

- Ask your potential new disciple:

  Please tell me, do you _____ to be discipled?

  Please tell me _____ do you want to be discipled?

  Will you commit to meet together until you are discipled and _____ to win someone to Christ and disciple them?

- I will now tell you when I received the Lord and how I became a discipler.

  We will now _____ complete the discipleship questionnaire and then exchange it with each other to get to know each other better (if it is the right time to do this with the new disciple).

- We agree to meet together.

  We will now set a day and time to meet every _____.

  Day:_____   Time:_____   Place:_____

  Visit www.TheJourneyForum.com to see more on this subject.

  Have your Discipler sign and date here when they review this assignment: This assignment was completed successfully.

  Date completed : _____ Discipler signature:_____

Conversation
LESSON 9

WITNESSING. MY TESTIMONY. SOLVING PROBLEMS. HEALING & TONGUES. COMMUNICATION. BEHAVIOR. WITNESSING. MY TESTIMONY.

SECTION A

Problem Solving

Key Objective: Learning to solve conflicts between each other.

Unfortunately, there will be times of offense, hurt and disagreement between Christians. We try not to offend anyone with our words, actions or attitudes, but it will happen and sometimes other Christians will offend us. If and when this happens, if it is _____ enough, the Bible gives these principles to follow:

- **Colossians 3:8-9**

  First, we must realize that these sins are no less serious in the eyes of God than any other sins.

- **Matthew 18:15**

  If we are offended, go directly to the other _____ first privately, and try to settle it between yourselves.

- **Matthew 18:16, 1st Corinthians 6:1-5**

  If the matter is not resolved privately, take it to a _____ in your church to help solve the problems.

- **1st Corinthians 6:6** Do not go to _____ people to settle a problem with believers.

- **1st Corinthians 6:7,8**

  If the matter still cannot be resolved: see if it's possible to personally _____ the wrong.

God provides answers to all of life's problems.

- **Colossians 3:13**

  How can I forgive others when I do not want to?

- **Ephesians 4:32**

  Forgive because Jesus asked you to. Forgive because _____ forgave all of your sins.

- **Romans 8:28**

  Forgive because you know that God uses all things for our _____. Forgive quickly. Seek forgiveness by humbly going to the other person.

SECTION A

How to avoid problems with people:

- **Psalms 119:165** Do your _____ in the Word everyday.

- **Proverbs 13:3** Learn to keep your mouth _____.

- **Proverbs 13:10** Remove _____ from your life.

My words affect my disciples.

- **Proverbs 15:28** Do not _____ about people.

- **Romans 12:10** Do not insist on your _____ _____ all the time.

In summary, there will be times when we offend others and they offend us. But the Bible gives us clear steps to follow to clear things up so we can focus on what matters most.

Visit www.TheJourneyForum.com to see more on this subject.

Reflect & Transfer
Take a moment to understand and learn so that you can share it.

What are the main points of this section? What part of this section stands out to you most? What questions do you have about this section? Are there parts of this section that you disagree with? How would you explain **Matthew 18:15-16**? Are there any verses we want to memorize?

Here's a "water cooler" scenario: A friend at work asks you, "If Jesus is so great, why are some of his followers such jerks?" How would you respond?

Here's another one: Your neighbor says, "I don't go to church anymore because there are so many hypocrites there." How would you reply?

Write **Ephesians 4:32** in the space below - going down a line at each punctuation mark.

_____
_____
_____
_____

How would you explain that verse?

SECTION B

False Teachers

Key Objective: To understand how false teachers work.

You can uncover false teachers and cults with a few simple questions: Do they believe in the biblical doctrine of the Trinity? Do they teach that Jesus Christ is not God? Do they teach any book other than the Bible? Do they add or subtract teachings from the Bible? Do they teach good works for salvation? Or do they teach any plan of salvation other than faith in Christ?

If the answer is "yes" to even one of these questions, it's very likely that person is from a false religion or cult.

- Read **1st Corinthians 2:2, Galatians 1:8**.

- **Matthew 7:15**

    Regarding false teachers, we are to _____ of them. Do not be deceived by them.

- **Acts 20:28-32**   Pray for your Pastor as he _____ out for false teachers.

- **2nd John 10-11**

    Do not receive them into your _____. Beware of those teaching religion on _____ and radio; many are false teachers and this is a way they come into your home.

I must be aware of deceptive teachers.

- **Acts 17:10-11**

    In this verse we see that the Bereans searched the Word of God daily. As we also continue in the Scriptures we can be aware of the deception of false teachers and false leaders, which is another reason to be Daily in the Word.

    In Lesson One, we were encouraged to know what we believe and how to draw people to Christ who are in non-Christian religions. Let's think about that again because today, you might see a Hindu family across the street or Muslims in the stores or Buddhists in the airport.

    The Mission Field has come to us! Are we prepared to share the truth of God's Word with genuine concern, drawing them to Christ?

    There are more resources at www.TheJourneyForum.com to equip you for your inevitable divine encounters with people of other religions - at school, at work, in your neighborhood, or even in your own family.

SECTION B

We have tools to help you respond with the unique truths of biblical Christianity to point them to Jesus Christ, to answer questions, and win souls for eternity.

Check the resources at www.TheJourneyForum.com regularly which include information on:

Knowing the Major Doctrines of the Word of God.
Major Religions in our world, such as: Catholicism, Islam, Buddhism, Hinduism, Judaism.
Major Cults in our world, such as: Jehovah Witnesses, Mormonism, Scientology and others.
Witnessing Tools like the Spiritual Map, Gospel Tracts, and more.

Reflect & Transfer
Take a moment to understand and learn so that you can share it.

What are the main points of this section? What part of this section stands out to you most? What questions do you have about this section? Are there parts of this section that you disagree with? How would you explain **Acts 17:10-11**? Are there any verses we want to memorize?

Here's a "water cooler" scenario: After you explain the Gospel to a friend, he says to you, "It's great that you found something that works for you." How would you continue to draw him to Christ?

Here's another one: An acquaintance asks you, "Why are Christians so homophobic?" How do you respond?

Write **Matthew 7:15** in the space below - going down a line at each punctuation mark..

_____
_____
_____

How would you explain that verse?

SECTION C

Words of a Disciple

Key Objective: Learning to draw people to God at the water cooler.

We were able to know the God of the Bible because someone took time and cared enough to bring the Gospel to us. Now, in turn, we have a responsibility to take it to others. This section teaches what the Bible says about witnessing.

Acts 1:8   We are called _____.

You have learned all but the last two steps of one on one discipleship. They are:

- **John 15:8**

    Step #7   A discipler leads people to Christ and disciples them. If we actively _____ people to Christ we will bring glory to God.

- **John 15:16**

    Step #8   A discipler multiplies disciplers who multiply disciplers. If we multiply disciple makers, we will fulfill God's _____ for our lives.

This is God's purpose for our lives and the purpose of your discipleship training. We are to lead people to Christ and disciple them to the point that they are prepared to lead people to Christ and disciple them. This process is to continue as long as we are alive.

I am to consistently draw non-believers to Christ.

1st Peter 3:15

Is any one asking you about Jesus? Your own personal salvation story is the greatest true miracle that ever occurred in your life. Your eternity was changed. It's your story, so no one can debate what happened to you.

Here is the concept in using your conversion story to witness for Christ: you answer simple, everyday questions with phrases that tell your story of becoming a Christian. How? You use simple "prompting" phrases in your conversations that include curiosity-creating words to encourage the hearer to ask more questions to move the conversation in a spiritual direction.

These "prompting" phrases show you are opening up your life in a personal way, especially when you say you were wrong about what you used to believe or you were wrong in how you lived, etc. The "prompting" phrases tell the person that you are being "real" and open the door to building a personal connection with them.

The "prompting" phrases help you to determine the progress of the Holy Spirit in that person's life. As they ask you for more information, you are gaining permission to tell them more and more of the Gospel, even if you only have a few minutes. Remember your goal is that they clearly know about the most

SECTION C

important decision they will ever face...salvation, the rest is up to them.

Your goal in the conversation is to:
1. Help bring a person to the point of acknowledging his one true need in life: God.
2. Increase his understanding of God's desire for his salvation and a relationship with him.
3. Present how he can experience salvation and that relationship.

Here are some "prompting" phrases to use to get questions to tell your conversion story:
... I had an experience ___ years ago that gave me a vision for my life and .... spiritual things didn't interest me much for most of my life, and then about _____ years ago, my perspective completely changed.

... it might sound kind of weird, but I once was considered _____ by most people's definition until something happened to change my mind. I was challenged to really pursue spiritual truth, and I discovered that my perspective on God was completely wrong.

Phrases to consider if they ask for more information: ...it's kind of personal, but I'm happy to share it with you if you really want to know.

If you are asked about your church or something related to church include phrases like: ... helps people understand spiritual perspectives on life. It's a lot of fun, and very thought provoking.

If someone talks about the sinful activity they did last night/weekend: ...I understand what you mean because I used to do that too, but about ___ years ago I had an experience that changed my perspective. Now everything is different. I don't miss that though.

Here are Phrases and questions to use as the conversation develops: ... what do you mean by Christian? ... what do you believe about God?

"Prompting" phrases include words like:
   Spiritual experience...
   I used to think that way too, but I had an experience __ years ago that changed my perspective...
   I discovered I was wrong...
   Life-changing experience...
   Change in belief...
   I had a spiritual experience that changed the direction of my life. Nothing has been the same since...
   My perspective about God changed when I ... now I think differently...

Discuss what other "prompting" phrases you can think of or that you have used.

- In sharing the story of your salvation:

   Make it personal. Tell what Christ has done for you. Keep Christ central. Always emphasize the Word of God. Your story should have these parts: Before I trusted Christ/ How I trusted Christ/ Since I've trusted Christ. Carry a small New Testament with you. When presenting Christ, let the other person read the verses for himself if possible.

- **Hebrews 4:12**

   What does God's Word say as it relates to witnessing?   When anyone hears the Word of God it speaks

SECTION C

to their heart. Remember God's Spirit is also speaking to the person's heart while you are speaking the Word of God to them.

- **2nd Timothy 2:23-26**   According to these verses, how should you handle a situation with a difficult or indifferent person?

- If you want to see more people come to Christ, put these simple activities into action:
  1. _____ people to hear the Word of God at your church every Sunday.
  2. Every week build relationships to the _____. They must see a genuine love and concern on your part for them.
  3. Use _____ to lead into spiritual conversations. Questions provoke thoughts.
  4. Give your _____ to someone every week.
  5. _____ the Spiritual Map and Lesson One. Practice with your Discipler. Show someone the Spiritual Map every day.

- Discuss the important facts about witnessing for Christ found in **1st Corinthians 2:4-5**. Remember, in witnessing, you have three powerful resources:
  The _____ of God - As you give out the Word of God it will supernaturally work.
  The _____ of God - He will help you witness and will work in every heart.
  The local _____ - The Word of God is preached and taught and disciples are made.

 **Reflect & Transfer** Take a moment to understand and learn so that you can share it.

What are the main points of this section? What part of this section stands out to you most?
What questions do you have about this section? Are there parts of this section that you disagree with?
How would you give your testimony of salvation that would use the method in this section?
Are there any verses we want to memorize?

Here's a "water cooler" scenario: You are witnessing to a neighbor and he says, "But there's so much evidence for evolution." How would you continue to draw him to Christ?

Here's another one: A co-worker says to you, "I've got several gay friends. I would say they're just like you and me. Being gay is just the way they were born." How would you respond?

Here's another one: You are witnessing to a family member and she says, "I would never tell anyone their religion is wrong." How would you continue to draw her to Christ?

Write **John 15:16** in the space below - going down a line at each punctuation mark.

_____
_____
_____
_____

How would you explain that verse?

SECTION C

Daily in the Word

Reading, Writing, Saying and Studying the Bible.

Your Discipler will now take a thorough look at all the sections in your Daily in the Word notebook and give instructions if needed. If you are Daily in the Word you will mature spiritually.

Don't forget that, when you finish **Mark**, start on **Romans** to **2nd Thessalonians**. When you finish those books, write Acts, and beyond that, continue until you write your own copy of the Word of God.

At The Journey Forum, there are other ideas for doing your Daily in the Word. You'll see other plans like these:

- Survey the Old Testament
- Survey the New Testament
- Survey the Life of Christ
- Read through the Bible in 30 days or 90 days.

Surveys are a combination of reading sections of the Bible, comparing Scripture and writing out key verses that you find.

More plans are being developed all the time that will help you with a life time of being in God's Word, so check the web site. The most important thing is that we put God first in our lives and we will if we are Daily in the Word.

Online Resources

TheJourneyForum.com

If you have a smartphone, you can download the lessons and other helpful material directly to your device.

Also, consider sharing with other disciples and disciplers how you are doing in your Daily in the Word. See The Journey Forum for more details.

Reflect & Review

Take a moment to understand and learn so that you can share it.

Question	Struggling	Needs Improvement	Growing	Doing Well
How are you doing in your Daily in the Word?				
How are you doing in memorizing the Word of God?				
How are you doing in your daily prayer time?				
Are you faithfully meeting with your Discipler?				
Have you been water baptized Biblically?				
Are you faithful to attend and give to your Local Church?				
How are you at sharing the Gospel with others?				
What is your commitment level to one on one discipleship?				
Are you preparing to have your own disciple?				
Can you teach the Spiritual Map?				
Can you give your testimony?				
Can you teach Lesson One?				

Mark the memory verses you have learned so far:

- ( ) Genesis 1:1
- ( ) Ephesians 2:4
- ( ) 1st John 5:7
- ( ) Isaiah 14:12-15
- ( ) Matthew 25:41
- ( ) Genesis 1:26-27
- ( ) Genesis 2:16-17
- ( ) Romans 5:12
- ( ) 10 Commandments
- ( ) John 11:43-44
- ( ) John 11:25-26
- ( ) John 14:6
- ( ) John 10:28
- ( ) Mark 8:36
- ( ) Luke 5:20
- ( ) Luke 7:48
- ( ) John 3:16
- ( ) 1st Cor. 15:3-6
- ( ) John 3:36
- ( ) Revelation 20:15
- ( ) John 20:31
- ( ) Romans 10:13

Date completed : _____ Discipler signature: _____

Assignments for Lesson Nine

1. With your Discipler, complete the Discipleship Training Module(s) on the following pages.

2. The disciple will present, teach and explain the Spiritual Map to one or more persons with the Discipler present. An appointment should be made with the person or persons to whom the disciple will teach the lesson.

Second, the disciple will present the Assurance Chart to someone with the Discipler present.

Important Note: You are close to finishing these lessons. At the end of these lessons you should be ready to lead someone to Christ and disciple them to do the same. Share the Spiritual Map with the lost so that you can begin discipling when you receive final approval from the church leadership and your Discipler. Have you led anyone to Christ?

Date completed : _____ Discipler signature: _____

3. Memorize and quote or write, at your next meeting, the 8 Steps of Discipleship as they are listed below.

   Step #1   Become a Believer by trusting Jesus Christ as Savior from John 3:16.

   Step #2   A disciple is in the Word of God every day from John 8:31.

   Step #3   A disciple is in prayer to God every day from Luke 11:1.

   Step #4   A disciple and discipler meet together every week from John 13:33-35.

   Step #5   A disciple is faithful in a biblical local church from Ephesians 4:11-12

   Step #6   A disciple is obedient to the Word of God and becomes a disciple maker from Luke 14:33.

   Step #7   A discipler leads people to Christ and disciples them from John 15:8

   Step #8   A discipler multiplies disciplers who multiply disciplers from John 15:16.

Date completed : _____ Discipler signature: _____

4. Write your "prompting" phrases and your testimony on paper (following the plan given in this lesson) this week and bring it to your Discipler at your next meeting. To get more resources for evangelism, go to www.TheJourneyForum.com including the Spiritual Map and Gospel Tracts.

Date completed : _____ Discipler signature: _____

Module 7

Your Strategy in Discipleship.

Work on this with your Discipler.

- _____ together and _____ together.

- View the commands in the Bible concerning a believers conduct toward _____ _____ as instructions for one on one discipleship.

- Sometimes you will not even _____ the lessons but talk about problems, difficulties, questions or something they _____ in their Daily in the Word.

- Get to know your disciple. Do not meet together and just go over the _____. Also, do not just _____. Keep a _____.

- These activities are part of one on one discipleship: appointments, fellowship, friendship, counseling, encouragement, loving correction, teaching, application, assignments plus others. But not all of these may be in _____ at every _____.

- The first three or four meetings with your disciple, you want to take your disciple's spiritual _____. Don't overwhelm a new believer at first with too much work or _____. Your disciple should be able to open his _____ to you.

- Your disciple must be a main _____ in your life. Lead your disciple. Make every _____ needed for your disciple. You are a pattern for your disciple. Have a life worth _____. Give time for your disciple.

- Take your disciple with you to some _____ activities. If you get through the lessons and do not have a _____ with your disciple, that is not one on one discipleship. It is not just the lessons that will produce a great disciple; you also need a close _____ with your disciple.

- You are to become very close to your disciple but the issue is _____ to Christ. The issue is not how many _____ or how many disciples you have, but how you are _____.

- Be patient. You are building a foundation that, if laid _____, will produce fruit that will remain. It takes _____ to reproduce correctly. And remember, you cannot be _____ to your disciple. Allow the Holy Spirit to lead and _____ you both.

Visit www.TheJourneyForum.com to see more on this subject.

Have your Discipler sign and date here when they review this assignment:
This assignment was completed successfully.

Date completed : _____ Discipler signature: _____

Loving God
LESSON 10

SECTION A

# Loving God

Key Objective: To understand where we go from here.

"Congratulations for getting to this lesson. It was our intention that your relationship would be deep and wide with God our Father and with each other from your time in His Word. Each of you are to have new disciples soon, if you do not already, but it's our desire that you will always remember the impact this time of discipleship has made on your life. In this lesson we cover some final thoughts about loving God, keeping our lives focused on Christ and those things that count for eternity. May God bless you in this lesson." John and Cathy Honeycutt.

The Greatest Commandment - Loving God

This section to be read by the Discipler to the disciple.

Jesus was asked what is the first or most important Commandment in the Scriptures. Read His answer in **Mark 12:30**.

His answer is to love God. But how can we see that true in our lives today?

- **How can we love God with all of our heart?**

Through our Personal Prayer: the first and most important step in growing in our love of God is our personal communication with Him. In prayer we speak and listen to God. As His disciples, we are to pray without ceasing. We speak to Him and listen for Him throughout the day; every day. Through our communication with God we come to know Him more and more. And as we know God we begin to understand His supremacy, holiness, and glory. The more we experience God in our life, the more gratefulness, thankfulness and love to God will be in our words to Him. God is love and to know God more is to love God more each day.

The Greatest Commandment...Love God.

- **How can we love God with all of our soul?**

Through our Worship: we can express our love to God by living for Him daily with a holy life and relating to other true Christians with hope, affection, and commitment. God has made the church His appointed place of worship today. Therefore, a disciple who wants to love God meets faithfully with other disciples for worship and prayer together. The first disciples quickly gathered together into a loving spiritual family. In the same way, we can do more together than apart in biblically expanding God's work. Worshipping together joins us, as His disciples, in more purposeful worship of God.

- **How can we love God with all of our mind?**

Through our Daily in the Word: reading, writing, saying and studying Scripture changes our lives into the people God wants us to be. Being Daily in the Word allows God to reveal Himself more fully and increase our enthusiasm and dedication. We are to approach Scripture with a willingness to learn; with a desire to have the Holy Spirit renew our minds according to the truths of God's Word. We believe that the Holy

Spirit lives within us and is actively transforming our lives. To grow in loving God, we must live daily in His strength - by the power of the Holy Spirit. As His disciples, we can express our love for God by reading Scripture faithfully, humbly, and with faith.

Through our Decisions: our decisions reveal our values and priorities. We can't make decisions based on what we want or what we think others want for us. Those disciples who have surrendered their lives to God ask Him "What do you want me to do in this decision?" We can love God by making decisions according to His will.

- How can we love God with all of our strength?

Through our Giving: another way to love God is by using our resources to serve Him. Loving God involves surrendering everything into His hands—including money and belongings. Tithing and giving cheerfully comes from a heart that knows God will take care of everything. As disciples we make an impact in expanding the Gospel around the world through our giving. Wise and generous handling of money is a tangible way of expressing our loving commitment to God. Let's love God by giving. The Bible says He "**loves a cheerful giver.**"

Through our use of Time: many believe that time is the new currency in our culture today. We often value and guard our time more jealously than anything else. So granting our time and energy to God is another realistic way to love Him. We should not spend all of our time in pursuit of personal leisure and recreation. It does take time to witness and develop a disciple to multiply, but it's time that will count for eternity. Let's keep one on one discipleship a high priority in our time commitments. Asking God every day to direct the concrete reality of our daily schedule is an important way to love God.

- How can we love God the way He should be loved?

Disciples should use all their time, money, and actions to serve and glorify God. Fortunately, God is so patient with us. We know that God does not need us; however, He has decided that He wants us. So, we must remember that we shall grow in our relationship with God as we are faithful. A disciple does not learn to love God totally in a short period of time. Growth in loving God is a journey and is tested at key junctures in our lives. For example, when we face hardships in our lives, we may become disillusioned with God or we may draw closer to Him. When we experience success or contentment in our lives, we may think it's our own abilities that are working or we may see those as God's blessings. How we respond to the workings of God's Spirit within makes all the difference.

What should we do now? Do what Jesus said in **Luke 9:23** and...take...it...a...day...at...a...time, "...If any man will come after me, let him deny himself, and take up his cross daily, and follow me."

A New Commandment   This section to be read by the disciple to the Discipler.

Jesus told us that the First Commandment is to love God, but did you know He also gave us a New Commandment in **John 13:34-35**? A new commandment I give unto you, That ye love one another; as I have loved you, that ye also love one another. By this shall all men know that ye are my disciples, if ye have love one to another.

- **Everything about the life of Jesus is an example and pattern for every one of us to follow.** His life instructs us today whether we are an individual Believer, a disciple, a Discipler or a Leader. He said love one another as I have loved you. How did He love His disciples? What was His example? The Bible says

SECTION A

LESSON 10 — Loving God

Jesus loved His disciples to the end. He spent most of His time training disciples. Remember that the Bible says He had a company of disciples from which He chose twelve to be with Him constantly. Among the twelve He made some of them leaders.

Now not all of us are called by God to lead and train a large group of people. And not all of us are called to train and direct leaders. But there is an example that Jesus gave that every one of us can follow; we all can have a one on one disciple like Jesus did. John, the "disciple whom Jesus loved" as the Bible calls him, is the one Jesus personally discipled. It's up to God whether He calls you to lead the way or the place He has for you in serving Him. But all of us are called to have at least one disciple whom we love, care for and mature to do the same with someone else.

- Jesus said the First Commandment is to love God. **The New Commandment Jesus gave is that we follow His example and be a disciple maker**. I'm sure we would agree that any Commandment in the Bible from God is to be taken seriously. And this New Commandment is no different than "Thou Shalt not take the Name of God in vain" or "Thou shalt not commit adultery" or "Thou shalt not kill." It's a commandment. But it should be a desire and not just a commandment. If you really care about serving God and care about your disciple, you will take time for your disciple and help them spiritually. It all boils down to what we really care about...what's first place in our lives. But we should remember it's also about being obedient to Christ's command to us. And if we always have one on one disciples, our lives will make a significant, eternal difference.

A New Command...Multiply Disciplers.

In Summary   This section to be read by the Discipler to the disciple.

In this lesson, we have seen the Greatest Commandment is to love God, and that our best future is in making multiplying Disciplers as Christ commanded and lived.

Let's grow daily in our love of God through prayer, through worship, through being Daily in the Word, through our decisions, our giving, our time, and in discipleship.

Now, in conclusion, let's think about the first moment of being with God in Heaven. At that moment we'll realize we don't have to pray to God like we used to, but instead we can speak with Him face to face. We'll realize we can worship Him personally and directly, we can hear Him speak His words in person, and that all our thoughts, decisions and impulses are finally perfect. It's impossible to comprehend the joy we will experience at that moment.

But the Bible records there are two times God has to wipe away our tears in Heaven. Maybe it's because we'll realize that every one around us is a saved child of God. We'll look around and see that there are no unreached people any more. We'll understand that we no longer can lead anyone to Christ. We'll realize that we can't get back the time we had. We can't disciple any more. We can no longer give of the resources we had on earth. Those resources are gone. Money, that we worry about so much, is gone forever. Time, that we protect so much, is gone forever. We'll realize the unreached people are gone for eternity. What will that be like?

Let's realize that only now can we give, reach the lost and multiply soul winning disciplers. And the day is coming when we will no longer have these opportunities. Knowing that day is coming, let's love God, win souls, and multiply Disciplers. May we use the time we have left to make a difference for our Saviour, Jesus Christ.

Final Approval

Your Discipler and your Pastor will now check these items with you.

You are daily in the Word and daily in prayer?	Yes ( )	No ( )
You have been Biblically baptized in your local church?	Yes ( )	No ( )
You are faithful to attend and give to your local church?	Yes ( )	No ( )
You completed and understand each discipleship lesson?	Yes ( )	No ( )
You completed all assignments in the Daily in the Word?	Yes ( )	No ( )
You are obeying the Word of God taught in the lessons?	Yes ( )	No ( )
You desire to keep your life pure and Christ first?	Yes ( )	No ( )
You can give your testimony and witness?	Yes ( )	No ( )
Will you seek to know and love God through His Word?	Yes ( )	No ( )
Will you seek to worship God?	Yes ( )	No ( )
You believe making disciples is what God wants you to do?	Yes ( )	No ( )
You believe you are to lead people to Christ and disciple them?	Yes ( )	No ( )
You have a Disciple?	Yes ( )	No ( )

√ **You officially complete Journey when you have your own disciple.**

Write the name of your new disciple _____

Approval to Disciple given by - * Both signatures are required

By your Discipler (signature) _____ Date _____

By your Pastor (signature) _____ Date _____

From John and Cathy Honeycutt: "Please email us and let us know you have finished these materials so that we can rejoice with you. We have a special gift for you. These lessons are the first of four levels of training. Get going with your new disciple and if you want to know and learn more, have your Pastor contact us about the additional levels. May God bless you as you help others navigate the exciting journey of multiplying soul winning disciple makers." John and Cathy Honeycutt - **gift@thejourneyforum.com**

What's Next?

- Prepare to testify in your church about the journey you just completed and your new disciple.
- Consider additional levels of ministry training - see your Pastor about this.
- Stay in touch with your Discipler and gain counsel from him/her as you disciple.
- Continue to learn how to be a better Discipler.
- Always have at least one disciple.
- Consider the Great Commission and be open to going anywhere God leads.
- Stay close to God and love God with all your heart, soul, mind, and strength.
- Visit www.DisciplethePlanet.com to see more opportunities.

Journey in One on One Discipleship

Here is a summary of the Steps and Destinations in our Journey

Steps of Discipleship

Step #1 Become a Believer by trusting Jesus Christ as Savior - John 3:16.

Step #2 A disciple is in the Word of God every day - John 8:31.

Step #3 A disciple is in prayer to God every day - Luke 11:1.

Step #4 A disciple and discipler meet together every week - John 13:33-35.

Step #5 A disciple is faithful in a biblical local church - Ephesians 4:11-12

Step #6 A disciple is obedient to the Word of God and becomes a disciple maker - Luke 14:33.

Step #7 A discipler leads people to Christ and disciples them - John 15:8

Step #8 A discipler multiplies disciplers who multiply disciplers - John 15:16.

The Destinations of Spiritual Formation

1. They **know** Christ as Lord and Saviour. **John 8:30**

2. They have an **assurance** of their salvation. **John 20:31**

3. They have a **thirst** for God's Word and **grow** spiritually. **John 8:31**

4. They **communicate** with God and **know** Him personally. **Luke 11:1**

5. They have been **scripturally** baptized and **exhibit** personal stewardship in a local church. **Eph 4:11-12**

6. They can **transfer** Biblical truths of Christianity in **everyday** life. **John 13:33-34**

7. They have come to a point of **forsaking** all to follow Christ. **Luke 14:33**

8. They **model** lifestyle **behavior** consistent with Scriptural teaching. **Romans 12:1-2**

9. They are **actively** drawing non-believers to Christ. **John 15:8**

10. They are effectively **reproducing** disciple makers one on one. **John 15:16**